D0985715

MAN,
THE DIVINE ICON

The Patristic Doctrine of Man
Made according to the Image of God

by George A. Maloney, S.J.
John XXIII Center for Eastern Christian Studies
Fordham University

Dove Publications
Pecos, New Mexico

140080

IMPRIMI POTEST:

Eamon Taylor, S.J.

Provincial, New York Province, Society of Jesus

May 1, 1973

NIHIL OBSTAT:

Herbert Musurillo, S.J.

Censor Librorum

DEDICATION

To the contemplatives of America, especially those of the Association of Contemplative Sisters who encouraged the writing of this work.

ACKNOWLEDGEMENTS

We are grateful to the Wm. B. Eerdmans Publishing Co. of Grand Rapids, Michigan, for their permission to quote from *The Ante-Nicene Fathers*, edited by the Rev. Alexander Roberts, D.D., and James Donaldson, LL.D. (American Reprint of the Edinburgh Edition), and from *A Select Library of Nicene and Post-Nicene Fathers of the Christian Church*, Second Series, edited by Philip Schaff, D.D., LL.D.. and Henry Wace, D.D.

Most of the New Testament passages were taken from *The New Testament*, translated by James A. Kleist, S.J., and Joseph L. Lilly, C.M. Copyright © 1956 by the Bruce Publishing Company and used by their permission.

CONTENTS

FOREWORD

Our world has suddenly become a relatively small place in which to live. Advanced technology and space exploration make it possible through various satellites for any part of the world to be present in our living room at this moment on T.V. In a short time, communications media can bring good news and reports of evil to all nations. The Gospel is being promulgated as never before in history. Jesus Christ is being proclaimed as Savior and Lord. Yet a keener sense of social responsibility is definitely required if we are to take full advantage of the many communications improvements.

To blow up bombs in the Orient today can cause a cosmic disaster in multiple dimensions. The waste products of one nation can easily become a pollution problem for another. And while some zealous persons may be deeply concerned and involved about solving our ecology problems, others continue to exploit the masses with all sorts of mind pollution. In and through all the dilemmas comes a rather clear message: we must learn how to really live together with one another; days of isolation seem to be coming to an end rather quickly.

Is it any wonder that the individualistic piety that many of us inherited should seem almost totally inadequate to meet the contemporary demands of brotherly concern? No doubt a "pie in the sky" type of heaven does have its merits as a temporary respite for a weary pilgrim. Yet the earliest and most orthodox teaching of the Church (its part of the apostles' teaching) has always encouraged us to look forward to the resurrection of our bodies and life in the world which is to come.

Perhaps a new appreciation for this pristine revelation might help modern man find a more relevant, rational meaning for living today. Not only does he need to be able to see himself and the meaning for living in terms of God rather than merely egotistical measurements. Most importantly, he needs a positive motivation for living his life well—NOW!

A man doesn't just do a good job of it here on the earth that he might then pass on to some heavenly reward. Such an eschatology would certainly urge him to get it over with as quickly as possible. It has little if anything of positive value to say to the variety of pessimistic influences already found within modern paganism. To side with the negative forces in opposition to this world may very well lead more and more people to give in to the self-destructive deviations found explicitly in those cultural realms of drug, alcoholic and sexual abuse.

Jesus Christ did not come into the world to condemn sinners or our present creation. He came that we all might have life and live it to the fullest (John 10:10). Our heavenly Father didn't create us as transient beings who are on their way toward becoming angels. What an identity crisis that would cost us! Our journey is more of a pilgrimage into a promised land, a new earth and sky, a new world made out of the substance of this old one. God has pledged that He will take the human and earthly condition for real for all eternity. This is why He sent Jesus to be Savior of the world. His own personal resurrection (His resurrected body is a transformed version of His earthly one: even the wounds were apparent—John 20:27) is a testimony for the entire universe that God is bringing about a new order of things.

Because of this pledge, the Father raising Jesus from the dead by the Holy Spirit's power, we Christians should not focus on some unearthly paradise to the degree that we fail to recognize our earthly responsibilities. The Gospel of Jesus Christ is made up of incarnational happenings or events which, when viewed as a whole, are the new earth and sky coming into being. A truly committed Christian should seek first his own personal transformation that he might then impart new life unto others. He should become a life-giving organism, filled and transfigured by the Holy Spirit, and then actively submit himself to be an active instrument that can be used for the transformation of other lives as well as this world. For God's Kingdom, which is already partly present amongst us, will come into its fullness as He reforms all present existing creation.

Our new earth and sky (Rev. 21) will be a transfigured version of our present earth and sky. How else could human persons live there, even with a glorified body? Today's scientific world seems to concur with this vision of transfiguration. Nothing in present world reality ever totally passes away; earthly substances know only transformation, not annihilation. In this transformative process that is presently going on, we human persons can either involve ourselves as part of the problem or as part of the solution.

Reminding people of this vision, their responsibility in reacting to the prophetic call of transformation, can help give them a sense of dignity, value and worth both on an individual and a communal basis. Only the magnitude of involvement that is demanded for a faithful response to such a vocation can give modern man the sense of destiny and sufficient challenge to cry out with his whole being to God for the grace to "live a life worthy of his Christian calling." Surely a part of that prayer can also be his daily work.

Through such an understanding we also probably find the best reason for writing and publishing this book, MAN, THE DIVINE ICON. Reading the early Church Fathers can help us formulate a healthy, Christian anthropology that might indeed give men a purposeful meaning for living well today. Their writings constitute a charismatic spirituality that is drawn from the lives of a people who were forced to live in a decadent society. Here we can find living examples of how real men of God understood themselves, their relationship with God, other people and the world about them. They remained faithful to the call of Jesus despite the difficulties that surrounded them.

The words of Ireneus, for example, still witness that "the glory of God is a man fully alive." We might wish to extend this by saying that "the glory of God is a people and universe fully alive" — recapitulated in Christ Jesus, our Lord! Such a vision is going to come true despite the difficulties that presently encircle us.

May these pages help to hasten that day by giving new hope to all of you who read them. May you become even more faithful workers in the Lord's harvest. And as you follow the Holy Spirit's promptings, may all your works invite the reign of peace upon our earth and the joyful return of our Savior and Master, Jesus Christ.

+David Geraets, O.S.B.

INTRODUCTION

IMAGE AND LIKENESS

Catholic, Protestant and Orthodox scholars feel that a Christian theological dialogue must begin on a patristic level. For all Christians the teachings of the early Fathers hold a strong appeal of authority. Their writings are also dressed out in biblical language which today forms the other common meeting ground among ecumenical-minded Christians. The Catholic Church has witnessed a flowering in its ranks of patristic research. One area that has occupied the chief attention of scholars is that which we can call a theology of the anthropology of man. Expressed summarily as the image doctrine or deification (*theosis*) or divinization, it is the central theme around which the early Greek Fathers constructed their theological speculation. Through a study of this central theme of the image among the Fathers we come into direct contact with their best theological thought on Christology, the Trinity, theological anthropology and psychology of man, a theology of creation and of grace, the problem of nature and supernature, a theology of the spiritual life and the laws of its development and progress.[1]

The early Fathers, in asking the question, what the nature of man is, turned to God and His divinely inspired word for the answer. "And God said, 'Let us make man according to our image and likeness.' "[2]

They did not see in this *speech* of God a similar imperative used by God to bring into being the sub-human cosmos: "Let there be . . . . and there was." The author of the book of Genesis was interpreted by the early Fathers as having indicated by divine inspiration a new creative act on the part of God which would set man off completely from the rest of creation. Michelangelo, in his famous

Sistine Chapel painting of God's creation of man, pictures God as descending and touching man. God creates man not as He does other things, already complete in their relationship of dependence upon God. Only man is created an *unfinished* being, one who in his first moments of existence immediately says a relation of person to person to God. Not only is man created by God through Him, but man is created in God and for Him. Man is to find his fullness in Another.

Serge Bulgakov described man's uniqueness over all other creatures to consist in his having been made by God to be a self-positing creature.[3] The image of God in man consists ultimately in possessing the spiritual faculties of intellect and will through which instruments man may posit himself as an *I*, dependent on the Absolute *I* of God. Genesis, as the early Fathers interpreted its story of the creation by God of man, indicates by the use of "Image and likeness" that man's total being has its meaning in the Prime Image of God, namely, the Logos, the Divine Word that mirrors forth as the Speech of God the incomprehensible Mind of God. God creates man not as a totally independent being but precisely as a self-positing being in reference to a Prototype. That Prototype is the Divine Word, the "Image of the invisible God," as St. Paul describes Christ[4] and according to which image and likeness (*kat' eikona kai kath' homoiosin*, as the Septuagint has it: Genesis 1, 26) man has been created.

Man therefore is not the image of God, but in his very being he says a relationship to God in and through Jesus Christ. Jesus Christ is the perfect Image. Man is made according to that Image. Emil Brunner beautifully describes this ontological relationship to God through the Word thus:

> God creates man in such a way that in this very creation man is summoned to receive the Word actively, that is, he is called

to listen, to understand, and to believe. God creates man's being in such a way that man knows that he is determined and conditioned by God, and in this fact is truly human. The being of man as an 'I' is being from and in the Divine 'Thou,' or, more exactly, from and in the Divine Word, whose claim 'calls' man's being into existence . . . . The characteristic imprint of man, however, only develops on the basis of Divine determination, as an answer to a call, by means of a decision. The necessity for decision, an obligation which he can never evade, is the distinguishing feature of man . . . it is the being created by God to stand 'over-against' Him, who can reply to God, and who in this answer alone fulfills—or destroys—the purpose of God's creation.[5]

In man's relations to the rest of creation the early Fathers picture him, in possessing an intellect and free will, as a king, a prophet and priest. He was the center, drawing all brute creation into its fullness by choosing to use all creatures *kat'eikona*, according to the Image, which is the Divine Logos, the Word that mirrors forth the Divine Mind.

But man failed to keep himself open to the living Word, the Speech of God showing man his greatness to consist in a loving submission to the Creator. Man sins by positing himself as an absolute *I* instead of a created *I* that finds his fulfillment in submitting to the living Word of God.

The Eastern Fathers divide themselves, unintentionally, into two camps in regard to the effects of sin on the image of God in man. One group, led by Irenaeus, consistently maintains a clear distinction between image and likeness. Sin could never destroy the image which was the ontological, spiritual principle of intellect and free will in man that contained as imperishable *seeds* an indeterminate response or openness to God's life. Yet sin, as a free, conscious response on man's part to turn away from God's life, destroys this ontological relationship of a community in the same life and love shared between God and man.

The other group, with St. Athanasius as the most consistent example, stresses the image of God in man as the *kat'eikona*, the ontological relationship in the life of God through grace between God and man, effected by God's loving condescension and man's habitual receptivity to God's living presence. Sin puts to death God's presence whereby man would have been assimilated by the sameness of the divine grace into a son of God by participation in the same life of the Son of God who is this by nature. In this sense the image of God in many can be destroyed.

It should be noted that the Fathers used this concept of image and likeness as a very fluid theological structure to describe the very real but mysterious communion in the same life between God and man. As the pages of this book will demonstrate, there is no agreed equivalent to these words; one must always study them in the context of the individual Father's writing. For this reason, I have tried to give a brief background of each Father studied so as to understand the milieu in which he wrote. I have tried to expose the reader to as many pertinent texts as possible, written by the Fathers chosen for this study, rather than impose my own ideas. In this way the reader can soon develop an insight into the patristic style of *theologizing*, one that has different starting points and methods quite strange to those of Western Scholasticism.

It is hoped that this study will unveil something of the riches contained in the ancient writings of the early Greek Fathers. I have ended with the writings of St. Cyril of Alexandria, not only because the pages had reached the measure of a good-sized book, but principally because after him we see no really new insights offered by the later Fathers in regard to our image-likeness doctrine. Maximus the Confessor, Pseudo-Dionysius, John Damascene and Gregory Palamas, all have written on this subject and have insisted on their loyalty to their patristic predecessors of the first five centuries.

In our modern age that is searching for a Christian anthropology of man that will recall to a secular society man's true dignity as seen from his Creator's viewpoint, the early Greek Fathers' presentation of the image-likeness doctrine breaks through any static conceptualization of man's nature. Karl Rahner's words nicely summarize the early Fathers' view of man as being created "according to the image of God": . . . to be a person is to possess oneself as a subject in conscious free relation to reality as a whole and its infinite ground and source, God."[6]

God is the ground of man's being. Man has been created by God's ever constant, never changing, present-now act of *love*. And man never lives outside the glow of this love. God is constantly ordering man towards a personal response of "Yes" to God's invitation that man become like to the Image that His Divine Son is. St. Paul phrases this thus: "You have put on the new man, that is being re-newed unto knowledge after the image of Him that created him."[7]

The ever-pursuing love of God does not destroy, in the Greek Fathers' eyes, the responsibility of man to answer God's invitation. Man is not like the in-animate creation but is a person, capable of knowing the Person God and responding in an act of sub-mission that is the most perfect expression of man's *creatured* love. In this the early Christian Fathers placed man's greatest dignity which, when fulfilled, made true the dictum repeated constantly from

Irenaeus down to all the other Eastern Fathers after him: "The Word of God was made a Son of man that man may receive the adoption and become a son of God."[8]

George A. Maloney, S. J.

Fordham University

CHAPTER ONE

THE PATRISTIC POINT OF VIEW

Man today, as always in history, can assume one of two predominant attitudes towards the world around him. The exploding universe with an accompanying sense of constant insecurity makes man feel the need for a stronghold of support. Yet the everyday violence, cataclysmic wars, evils that belch forth continually from our teeming cities, all these tend to create in him a black pessimism towards his world. Fear gradually seizes him and he sees despondency as the only alternative to a hopeless situation.

The other position is based on hope that springs from a belief in a God more powerful than man. It mounts to a powerful current of living hope in the Christian belief that this God is a tender, loving Father. "The Lord is my light and salvation. Whom should I fear? The Lord is my life's refuge. Of whom should I be afraid? Though an army encamp against me, my heart will not fear" (Ps. 26). This hope is based more perfectly on the conviction that God is all-loving and on the greatest manifestation of His love, that He poured Himself out for mankind by actually becoming a man.

"God is love. God's love was made manifest among us by the fact that God sent his only-begotten Son into the world that we might have life through Him."[1] St. John's summary of God as being by essence love and life provided the Eastern Fathers with their unique approach to the spiritual life. The love of God is the ground of man's being. Before the Fathers could speak of an anthropology of man, they had to speak of God from whom man came. The spark could be known only by the

1

Flame. Shared life could be understood only through a glimpse into Life itself. Man's self-realization through love would be possible only because "God is love and he who abides in love abides in God and God in Him."[2] Man is the overflow of God's fullness. In His utter selflessness because He was All, God's goodness created man, not to receive a needed love in return, but in order to pour out of the infinite abundance of His Being shared-life-in-love. This mystery, revealed to us by the Eternal Word of the Father, assures us that we have been made by God out of love, in love and destined for love by participating in God's own life.

Genesis provided God's own version of man's beginning: "And God said, 'Let us make man according to our image and likeness'"[3] The simple words *image* and *likeness* (*eikon* and *omoiosis*) provided the early Christian writers with an analogy around which they developed their best theological thought on Christology, the Trinity, creation and grace, the problem of nature and supernature, the laws of the spiritual life and its development and progress. But before we can develop the patristic theme of image and likeness of God in man, we must first see some of the particular points of emphasis common to the Eastern Fathers. The riches contained in their theological writings will remain always hidden to Western minds if they approach the patristic writings with their own thought categories, their own definitions of common words such as nature, grace, supernatural, etc. For most of the Fathers our thought categories were utterly unknown, as well as our philosophical foundations for theological speculations; hidden to them were our special problems and our tendency to view revealed truth in a vacuum instead of in the light of the dynamic order of salvation that is being effected in God's ever present *now*.

Finite man tends to view the unfolding of his life through historical time and space in three dimensions. Length, breadth, and depth are measurements made possible by beings immersed in matter. Thus time (past, present and future) and space or place are the square boxes into which we divide all of our human experiences. Our relationship to God is then described in similar terms. That God is Love and Life is soon relegated to a God before Creation, a God during Creation and a God after Creation. Our response to Divine Love's invitation is soon measured exclusively by extrinsic rules or moral laws of conduct.

The Eastern Fathers, because they were close in time and experience to the pristine message of the Gospel, had the unique quality of piercing through spatial and temporal concepts by viewing the history of salvation, man's relationship to God, not from man's myopic point of view, but from the all-encompassing view of God almighty. This *fourth-dimensional* perspective viewed God's extra-Trinitarian activity as a unity, unfolding it is true in time and space, but a oneness due to the same love that remained constant. It was God's infinite love that initiated the first act of creation and it is the same dynamic divine love evolving this initial creation into the fullness of His plan when the whole universe would be finally amorized into the "new creation" foretold by St. Paul: "If, then, any man is in Christ, he is a new creation; the old state of things has gone; wonderful to tell, it has been made over, absolutely anew! All this comes from the action of God, who has reconciled us to himself through Christ and has entrusted us with this ministry of reconciliation. We know that God was truly reconciling the world to himself in Christ, not reckoning against men their sins and entrusting to us the message of reconciliation."[4]

A modern thinker, Teilhard de Chardin, was aware of this fourth-dimensional perspective of the early Fathers. He strove in all his theological writings to return to the simple view of the early Christians by cutting through a static concept of God's activities in this universe. "In spite of the affirmations of Paul and the Greek Fathers, the universal power of Christ over Creation has up to the present time been little considered by theologians and then principally under the extrinsic and juridical aspect."[5] For Teilhard as well as for the Eastern Fathers, the same act of infinite love of the Trinity towards man was unfolding in the Creation, Incarnation, Redemption and will be unfolding in the final consummation of the total universe. To replace anthropomorphic pluralism of decrees on the part of God by the one ever *now* act of love, merely unfolding itself in space and time that cannot in any way change the quality of love for man, this was Teilhard's mission. And this was the unique facility of the early Fathers to view the total plan of the economy of salvation from the masterplan of God's will-act. The Fathers read Holy Scripture from God's viewpoint, thus they were able to transcend any progression that depended on time or place for its realization. God's salvific will was the beginning, the middle and the end of man's history on this earth.

MORAL REALISM

Thus God became for them the point that rooted man in being, and God's purpose in acting at all was the touchstone to reality. God was the *really real* for the early Christians, and everything else created participated in reality in the proportion that that creature mirrored forth the mind of God in its regard. The mind of God was discovered by contemplating the *logos* that lay, as the principle of harmony and relation of creature back to Creator, beneath the exterior appearances of sense knowledge,[6] The *logos* is therefore the *raison d'etre* of each creature or event, but viewed according to the economy of salvation of the Creator. To penetrate beneath the surface of sense impressions and to perceive the inner logos of a given creature was to know its place and role in the fulfillment of God's salvific designs. This is more than the ideas of Plato which always remained subsistent, static entities, removed from the all-perfect One, the Good. The logos according to the Greek Fathers was the nature of a being lived to its fullest potencies as not only willed by God in the first act of the creature's coming into existence, but as actuated by the constant activity of God upon that creature to attain His purpose. Inanimate objects had to exist according to their God-given logos. Man, with free will, had the ability to live according to the image according to which God had created him; or he could destroy the logos within him by living contrary to the mind of his Creator. In this sense, the most really real person was the one who was living constantly according to the mind of God, fulfilling the image according to which God had modeled him. The unnatural man was the independent person, living according to his own selfish interests; he was not fulfilling the logos, the full nature, as God had intended.

The Fathers can teach us a much needed lesson in realism by recalling us to their basic view of faith that saw all created being according to the plan of God. Herein lies one of the great differences between modern men and early Christians. Today we distinguish between the physical and the moral order. The physical, that which we can touch, taste, hear, see, smell, partakes of the greatest reality; it is the most real for us; while the moral order, the spiritual, is interpreted as something ideal rather

5

than real, mental, etherial, abstract, vague, nebulous rather than certain, solid and concrete. We speak today of moral forces and values, but the stress is on the material results that can come from actuating such.

The greatest reality that Jesus Christ came to reveal to the world, in the eyes of the early Christians, newly converted Jews and pagans, was that God so loved the world that He gave us His only begotten Son.[7] And this Living Word came that we might have God's own life and have it more abundantly.[8] The whole universe had its meaning, its logos, only in and through the Divine Logos. Man's full nature was man in whom the Logos lived. Origen puns on this word and concept of logos. Man is truly *logical* (*logikos*), a truly rational being according to all his powers, only by becoming a participator of the Logos. The holy person alone is truly logical for he alone truly fulfills his rational nature, which has been made by God according to God's Image which is Christ, the Divine Logos. The sinner, on the other hand, is a soul inhabited by the devil (*a-logos*, without Christ) and hence, though still retaining a rational nature, is not living according to his fullest potencies which destine him to be a true son of God by participation in the life of the Son of God who is divine by His nature. The sinner is both irrational and unfaithful to the element that makes him most essentially a man. He remains *without-the-Logos*, having lost the image of Christ through sin.[9]

IMAGE AND LIKENESS

Jesus Christ, therefore, for the early Christians, as well as for all Christians of every age, is the greatest reality, "yesterday, today and always" as St. Paul asserts.[10] Our creation according to His

6

Image and our deification according to His Spirit are in the moral order but are nonetheless real. For Plato the end of man was *homoiosis theou kata to dunaton*,[11] to approach to a likeness of God as far as possible. All intelligibility, all sensible realities were conceived by him as images of eternal models, the Divine Ideas. The sensible world mirrored forth the "image of the intelligent God."[12] The participated image tended to rediscover itself, to rejoin the ideal model by a liberation from the sensible world of matter and finally to arrive at an assimilation with God as far as possible.

The Greek Fathers found a Hellenic philosophy waiting to give expression to a reality that their pagan ancestors, even Plato, could never have dreamed of. Genesis assured them that God had made them according to His image and likeness. St. John told them, "We are sons of God, even now."[13] St. Paul confirmed their belief that "Through faith in Jesus Christ you are all now God's sons."[14] Irenaeus, Clement of Alexandria, Origen, Athanasius, the Cappadocian Fathers, Basil, Gregory Nazianzen and Gregory of Nyssa, Methodius of Olympus, John Chrysostom, Cyril of Alexandria, Maximus the Confessor and John Damascene, to name only a few of the leading Greek writers, developed a doctrine of the image and likeness of God in man. For them, as well as for St. John the Evangelist and St. Paul, Jesus Christ is the Logos, the archetype image of the many other images of God called men.[15] Not only is He the model according to which all things have been made, the exemplary cause, but He is also the instrumental cause which brings about the deifications whereby God declares: "God you are, I myself have declared it; you are favored children, every one of you, of the Most High."[16] Jesus Christ had told His followers: "I am the Way, the Truth and the Life. No one comes to the Father, but by me."[17]

Thus man's fullest meaning, his fruition, does not reside in himself but in Another. All the Fathers agree that man has been made according to Christ "in whom we have redemption, the forgiveness of sins; who is the image of the invisible God, the first-born of all creation, for by Him all things were created in the heavens and upon the earth, the visible and the invisible things, whether Thrones or Dominations or Principalities or Powers. All have been created through him and for him. He exists prior to all creatures, and in him they are all preserved in being."[18] Origen paraphrased Paul's doctrine of Christ, the perfect image of His Father and the model of man's imitation: "What was the image of God that man was modelled on? It could only have been our Savior. He is the firstborn of every creature (Col. 1,15). He said of Himself: 'To see me is to see Him who sent me' (Jn. 12,45) and again 'Whoever has seen me has seen the Father' (Jn. 14,9). If you see a picture of someone, you see the person the picture represents. Thus, when we see the Word of God, who is God's picture, we see God Himself."[19] And again he says: "All who come to him and strive to be like him are inwardly renewed, day by day, according to the progress they make, in the image of Him who made them."[20]

Man stands in the universe as the center of creation, the *opus Dei*, God's chef d'oeuvre. Brute creation must be the nature God intended; there is no choice. Only man is capable of opting to "be perfect as your heavenly Father is perfect."[21] By his creation according to God's image, man contains in his intellect and will the faculties of hearing God's invitation, His *appel*, as Henri de Lubac, S.J. calls it.[22] to answer God's Word within him in order to put on the life of Christ. Thus God does not impose as a task, but freely gives man, as a gift, the opportunity, the responsibility to return to God the love that He has first had for man. God has constituted man a total entity distinct from Himself, an *I* that will be complete only in relation through loving submission to a greater *Thou*. The mood is not the imperative command of a law, a duty, a "Thou shalt not" or a "Thou shalt" but is indicative, pointing out God's goodness; "Thou art mine, if thou wishest."

The following chapters will be an attempt to present the doctrine of the Greek Fathers concerning the Image and Likeness of God in man. As a preliminary, to appreciate the patristic language and approach we must touch briefly on two fundamental topics that lay at the basis of the Fathers' use of the image and likeness analogy. The first is the opposing emphasis among the Greek Fathers of viewing the end of man's spiritual perfection as a participation of God as Life or as Light. Another way of saying it as the opposition between the Semitic approach among the early Christians of encountering God as a total experience of Life and that of the Hellenic, speculative school of Alexandria of meeting God only through intellectual contemplation. The second topic is the understanding the Fathers had of human nature and its relation to the supernatural.

EXISTENTIALISM VS. ESSENTIALISM

Much has been written about the characteristics of the Semitic and the Hellenic cultures.[23] The Semitic approach is considered dynamic, voluntaristic, existential, psychological, while the Hellenic emphasis is static, intellectual, essential, logical. It is true, at least, that the Semitic Jews received Divine Revelation through God's Word pronounced and then listened to by the Chosen People. In the Old Testament there are visions, but these serve only as background for God to reveal Himself through a communication of words. Moses at the burning bush hides his eyes from a vision of God but encounters God through what he hears.

The pagan Greeks, on the other hand, possessed to a high degree the gift of seeing and contemplating. Truth was not heard, it was seen and contemplated in the eternal Ideas. Knowledge is according to the analogy of visual perception. Intelligence, the *nous* of man, is the center of all knowledge, but to know is first to have seen. The object of knowledge for the Greek philosophers of the Platonic school is the perception of the essence of things, the idea which has the same name as the exterior image, the *eidos*. The idea is not a product of the mind but an image perceived by the spiritual eye, the intellect.

In the Old Testament life is the greatest gift given man by God. It is more than mere existence but contains the promise with the possibility of growing in fuller happiness, joy and peace. Life, in Hebrew *Hajjim,* was conceived by the sacred writers of the Old Testament as length of days, the full, good life;[24] it was joined with the possession of the land;[25] true life was opposed to life in Sheol, mere existence in the land of shadows;[26] finally it connoted the individual life after death with punishment or reward.[27]

Of the 133 times that the word life is used in the New Testament, St. John uses it 64 times. This clearly indicates his emphasis on union with God here in this life and in the life to come. He ends his Gospel with the summation: "But these things are written that you may believe that Jesus is the Christ, the Son of God, and that believing you may have life in His name."[28] Such a strong emphasis placed on life by an intimate of the Master Himself would indicate that the theology of life was a true Semitic interpretation of Christ's message.

The early Christian documents transmitted this theology of life in their expression of faith, the sacra-

10

ments and the ascetic life. Faith is the germ of life; to preach the Gospel is to sow the word of life. The new life is given in baptism which is not conceived as an illumination of the intellect but rather as a return to life.[29] Salvation was conceived as a new life "in Christ" with Christ as the life-giver. The sacraments were "carriers" of Divine Life. The early Christians in whom Jesus Christ dwelt with His own divine life were called by St. Ignatius of Antioch "vehicles of Christ" (*Christophori*) and Carriers of God Himself (*Theophori*).[30]

There can be shown a gradual development of the emphasis on contemplation with a diminishment of a total experience of the whole man with God through Grace, beginning even in the Old Testament. David's son, Solomon, had many contacts with Hellenic letters and this influence is evident in the sapiential writings of the Hellenized Jews of Alexandria. Wisdom soon replaces Life. "Wisdom is a tree of life for whoever seizes it."[31] Werner Jaeger has pointed out the influence of the Greek *paideia* and Hellenic culture in providing thought patterns and categories of thoughts, inherited metaphors and subtle connotations of meaning for the early Christian philosophers and theologians seeking a medium to express the message of Christ.[32] Gradually the message of St. John's Gospel with its strong accent on Christ as Life of our souls is seen merely as the primitive message to be speculated about in intellectual concepts rather than a total experience in Grace-life.

Gnosticism with its emphasis on the gnosis opened only to an esoteric few initiates into the Christian mysteries was combatted by Clement of Alexandria and Origen by a Christianity that was expressed in similar language. Salvation for the intellectual, speculative school of Alexandria consisted in the Christian gnosis, an intellectual contemplation that brought about union with God on the principle of "like assimilates like." From Origen contemplation as the end of the Christian life passed on to Evagrius of Ponticus, the speculative theologian for the Byzantine mystics. "The state of prayer is a passionless state, in which supreme love transports on high a wisdom-loving, spiritual mind."[33] God was to be *seen* by the intellect of man turning within itself; through grace God would reveal Himself in the flaming light of contemplation. The Byzantine Hesychasts would follow this tendency of flight from the material universe to find God in the interior of the soul. Gregory Palamas developed the theology of God's uncreated Energies around the inner Light that became the goal of all contemplation.

The Semitic tradition was kept alive with its emphasis on a total experience of the life of God in grace, known only through faith, by the Antioch school of Ignatius, Polycarp, Irenaeus, St. John Chrysostom. Among the non-speculative ascetics of the desert who followed Macarius' emphasis of the heart rather than the intellect, a spirituality of personal, warm devotion to Jesus, centered around the recall of His holy name (later to be incorporated into the so-called Jesus Prayer) developed that focused attention more on the person-to-person relationship between the individual and Christ living in the soul rather than an encounter that occurred only on the intellectual level. As opposed to Evagrius and his mysticism of light, Pseudo-Dionysius developed his mysticism of darkness where God revealed Himself as an intuitive experience in faith of God as Being, Life, Totality rather than as Knowledge.

It is dangerous always to draw too sharply the lines separating these two general emphases of life and contemplation, Semitic and Hellenic. But in order to view the remarks that the Greek Fathers made about the image and likeness we must keep ever present these two approaches. Certainly the emphasis of salvation as knowledge and its acquisition through contemplation was made by the Christian writers in contact with Hellenic philosophy as a way to adapt to the context and milieu of Hellenic culture. It is true that writers such as Clement of Alexandria, Origen and Gregory of Nyssa used Neo-Platonism as an instrument to explain Christianity to a public that knew no other thought categories. But there always was the danger, especially among their followers who did not distinguish as clearly as the masters, that something of the pagan philosophy or culture would affect the pristine Christian message with an emphasis that would not be essential nor even desirable and in some cases might be harmful. One such emphasis taken over by the Alexandrian intellectual school was the Platonic dichotomy that severed the sensible world from the really real world of the intellect. Man was principally a soul, or more precisely, the higher part of his soul, the intellect, while the body was looked upon as a drag, a consequence of sin. Man's realization came in suppressing the material of the body and releasing the spiritual of the intellect to contemplate a reality that existed beyond this present world. With such an emphasis on intellectual contemplation, a spirituality of flight from encountering this present universe and becoming a leaven to the masses to effect St. Paul's "new creation" could and actually did result throughout the Byzantine world. One could forget that this life is made to merit the vision of God through works done out of love for God, much more than to enjoy this vision now in repose or in a state of Stoic impassibility. There is some truth to the reproach made by Vladimir Soloviev that Eastern Orthodoxy was too willing to engulf itself under the guise of contemplation in a somnolent passivity and forget its Christian commitment to be the light of the world and the salt of the earth.

13

The West has suffered also from the thought categories taken from Neo-Platonism by Augustine and inserted into Western theology and spirituality. But when Western schoolmen no longer were mystics like the earlier theologians who could discourse on contemplation and never separate it completely from God as Life, theology fell into a rationalization of man's anthropomorphic view of God. It forgot to view God from God's view as revealed in Holy Scripture and as commented on by the early Fathers in their fourth-dimensional view through God's revealed Word. Moral theology developed as a special and necessary branch of theology, but the temptation was always present to view its work as simply to make laws guiding the maximum Christians to do the minimum necessary in order to be saved. Christianity became no longer an encounter between I and Thou, the neighbor, through the life of the Living Word in us but a set of extrinsic laws of moral conduct. Grace became a thing to be amassed and stored up in some heavenly bank as security against the day of reckoning, instead of the Trinity living within us, working dynamically to divinize us and through us to bring the Incarnation and Redemption to the world. The greatest obstacle to spiritual progress was the conception of man's life as a two story building. On the first floor was man with a full human nature, all that came to him from God in creation, including the effects of the sin of the first man, Adam. Man acted purely as a human being on this level, with the seeming implication that God was not too interested in this area except for the one faculty, man's will. This was the backstairs that led up to the second floor, the superimposed supernatural life. Grace builds on nature and God gratuitously gives His gifts to a receiving human nature that is disposed to receive them. Thus an individual could live in two different compartments, at one time a purely "natural" life and again a supernatural life in the state of grace. This brings us to the view of the Greek Fathers on nature.

NATURE AND SUPERNATURAL

Father de Lubac, in his much discussed book *Surnaturel*, seeks to show that the early Fathers, with their dynamic approach based on the concrete, historical human nature, the only one that now exists, had never admitted a nature that was not at the same time by its very ontological makeup, as it came from the hand of God, dynamically in movement towards its supernatural end.[34] It would be wrong to assert that the Fathers denied the possibility of a pure nature, a human nature not having God as its final end. The Greek Fathers simply never thought of the problem, absorbed as they were with the historical order of the present economy of salvation; and this shows us further their sense of *realism*. Not faced with the Pelagian heresy, as was St. Augustine, who bequeathed his important and subtle distinctions to Western theology to highlight the gratuity of God in being free and independent in His bestowal of graces on man, the Greek Fathers viewed the inter-relationship of nature and grace in terms of one continuous unfolding process of two different but not contradictory entities: man's ontological nature as God made him, with potencies that would be actuated with God's help only when the end was attained that God had destined for man; and God's gratuitous bestowal of the gift of Divine Life that drew out of the image according to which God created man a more perfect similitude to the perfect Image of God, the Divine Logos.

What was the common understanding of the Fathers when they used the word *nature* (*physis*)? The characterization of nature and grace as op-

15

posites described in the *Imitation of Christ*[35] where nature is depicted as being corrupt and tending always to vice, while grace is the elevating, infused force that allows the spiritual man to do good, would never have come from the pen of an Eastern Father. Their starting point was different. Fundamentally, nature for the Fathers is the *opus Dei* as it comes from the hands of God. This work of God, with all of its hidden, unactuated possibilities, as Irenaeus, Origen, Gregory of Nyssa and the other Greek Fathers repeat constantly, is good. There is nothing in man's makeup that is evil.

But the nature of man partakes also of the end that the Creator had in mind in giving it existence. God did not create a nature in a vacuum but created for it an end towards which the nature tends through the free-will cooperation of man with the Creator. A simple anecdote of the Fathers of the Desert illustrating this optimism of human nature conceived as an image of God is found in the *Vitae Patrum*.[36] A spiritual father was asked by a certain soldier whether God receives a penitent sinner back. The old monk gave many arguments to show the loving mercy of God towards His creature but finally said: "Tell me, friend, if your cloak is ripped, do you throw it away?" "No; of course not. I sew it and use it again," replied the soldier. "If therefore," answered the elder, "you have mercy, sparing your own garment, do you not think God is indulgent towards His own image?"

The whole man, body with all of its senses and passions, the soul with its intellect and will, all were created good by God. The whole scope of the spiritual life is to make a given, concrete human nature approximate that nature intended by God in His will-act of giving existence to it. Thus *nature* for the Greek Fathers is never a universal, abstract concept that can be applied equally to all humans in a static, self-composed, independent existence, but it

16

refers always to an ontological, existing being according to the given potencies and the plan of God with all of His graces given to a concrete person in order that he might fulfill God's salvific designs in his regard and thus attain his own perfect, *natural* self-realization.

In the Western concept of man's nature, man has animal and intellectual life; through a supernatural elevation (hence something outside and above nature) which is added to man's human nature, man's nature becomes changed, now assumes a different life with powers capable now of different operations, God-informed actions. Thus supernatural grace elevates man's *natural* nature and makes it now a supernatural nature. But, as has been said, nature among the Greek Fathers admits of a wider meaning. Emile Mersch writes: "It will be well to note that the term *natura* (or *physis*) which they (the Fathers) use so freely, does not correspond exactly to our word *nature*. It often has a vague, general meaning; to render the thought we have found no better word than reality and its derivatives."[37] Irenaeus constituted man's nature as composed of three parts: the body, the soul and the spirit. This was man in God's first creation and the ultimate way God had planned all men to be. This is the *logos* of his nature, the real nature of man. But Adam by his sin lost the spirit that had been given to him in an embryonic form to be developed progressively more unto the fullness of a son of God by Adam's free-will cooperation with the goodness of God. To give back what Adam had lost, the Son of God became man, taking on Himself our *nature* in the fullest sense of the word, body, soul and spirit, fully actuated in the being of the perfect Son of God.

Father Jean Danielou, S.J., points out well that St. Gregory Nyssa (and in this his influence has been the greatest of all Eastern spiritual writers) never distinguished between the intellectual life and the supernatural life. Both made up man's nature, which was created in the image of God; hence everything in it was good. The distortion that introduced into man's nature the seeds of dissension, disorder and sin could not have been found in any way in man's nature. It had to come from outside man.[38] The supernatural grace added to man in his re-generation into the new man by the reception in Baptism of Divine Life is not something superimposed, but, according to the Fathers, it is the actuation of a potency that was there in the nature from creation. All good that can come to man must be "according to nature" (*kata physin*). Vices or sins are the only things against nature, hence, unnatural, while the supernatural is eminently conformed to nature. Christian perfection of a virtuous life in grace does not do violence to nature, but it heals it, makes it grow, divinizes it without demanding any other sacrifice than the uprooting of a will that goes against the creative will of God. Only a free will act on the part of man is demanded by God in order that man receive the gifts of God that are contained in his nature as a seed contains all the perfections of the matured tree. Irenaeus has an apt expression: "Man is the receptacle of the goodness of God." If man consents by humbling himself to his true ontological place as a creature before his Creator, if he makes himself supple and malleable in the hands of the Divine Artist, God can make of him His chef-d'oeuvre.[39]

Thus we are brought back to the beginning of this chapter, "God is love." God spills out His love in activity in the creation of men and the universe, in the Incarnation of His Divine Son, Jesus Christ, in the Redemption by the God-Man of the whole human and subhuman cosmos, in the sanctification and final Parousia through the Holy

Spirit. These are all actions of God prompted by the one constant act of love.

Love, in order to exist, must always be loving, always pouring itself out from its own abundance, always giving of itself. It is thus through God's action of His loving us (and this we call grace) and in and through His life in us by our loving in return that we come to union with Love Himself. And in this oneness of Love, we are united with every other human being created and loved by God. The nature of God is such that while being one, it demands a plurality, a many, as objects of His love, of His giving. Love is the best word that St. John and any human being could choose to describe God's relation to man. In man's constant response to this invitation of God's love consists all his greatness and fulfillment. It is our loving in return (always made possible through God's grace) that divinizes us, brings us into a oneness in love so that God truly lives in us by participation. "God is love and he who abides in love abides in God and God in him." Grace therefore is God loving His human creation and deifying it through His activity with human beings freely choosing the Way to the Truth that leads to Life that is Love Personified.

With this as background we can study the doctrine of the early Greek Fathers concerning the image and likeness. To have begun without this framework would have given us an impression of vague, poetic indefiniteness on the part of the early Christian writers towards such a vital and concrete subject as grace, God's life in us. There has not been a Greek Father who has not expressed in similar terms what St. Irenaeus first expressed so succinctly when he wrote: " . . . For this is why the Word of God is man, and this is why the Son of God became the Son of Man, that man might possess the Word, receive adoption and become the son of God.[40] One must begin with the Word of God for He is the Alpha, and we will end with Him for He is the Omega. St. John tells us in his Prologue that all things were made through Him and without Him was made nothing that was made. To understand how man was made to God's image and likeness we must first study God's perfect Image, the Divine Logos. It is only in this ontological relation to the Word of God that man can understand his being in God for "He is the image of the invisible God, the first-born of every creature, because in Him were created all creatures . . . ."[41]

CHAPTER TWO

CHRIST—THE LOGOS, IMAGE OF THE FATHER

"And this is eternal life, that they may know Thee, the only true God and Jesus Christ whom Thou hast sent."[1] Theology, strictly speaking, for the Oriental Christians has always been conceived as knowledge about the Holy Trinity. To know this mystery revealed to us by God Himself is to enter into a union with God. But this is not to be a rational, discursive knowledge, arrived at by our own human efforts, but, rather, after a proper purification of the obstacles impeding union with God within us, God reveals Himself to us through a knowledge in direct experience. Theology thus is a growing encounter with God and His vital activities within us whereby man progressively changes, or better, God evolves human beings into "partakers of the divine nature."[2] These words of St. Peter are no empty analogy but are at the center of the revealed Christian message.

But from the revealed word of God in the Old and New Testaments and in the living tradition of the Church through the centuries, the divine nature is considered as inaccessible, uncommunicable to man. Any relation between God and man would seem to be at best only a figure of speech. This is the awesome, transcendent God of majesty appearing to Moses at the burning bush, the God of Isaias' vision who receives the constant praise of the trisagion from the six-winged Seraphim who cover their faces with their wings out of reverence.

Etiénne Gilson has expressed this foundation-stone for all human relationship with God thus: "Lower even if only for an instant and at one given point the abyss between God and man created by the contingency of creaturehood and you have taken away from the Christian mystic his God and hence his mysticism also. Any God who is not inaccessible, man can dispense with. It is the God who is by His nature inaccessible whom man cannot do without."[3] Yet Christ Himself promises that this inaccessible God, with the life of the Trinity, will descend and enter into our souls. "If a man has any love for Me, he will be true to My word; and then he will win My Father's love and We will both come to him and make Our continual abode with him."[4]

The Eastern Fathers, true to the basic belief in Christianity, saw Jesus Christ as the solution to this antinomy. Thus any discussion of the inaccessible God and the immanent union with His creature-man must start, as the Fathers did, with the Divine Logos, the *Logos endiathetos*, the interior language or speech of God applied to the *Verbum* in His divine, eternal existence, and move out through the Trinitarian *ad extra* activities into the created cosmos of men and things to the *Logos prosphorikos*, the spoken or pronounced word, that is, the Word Incarnate.[5]

Thus this chapter will treat of the evolution of a theology of the Logos, the Word, especially as seen in the writings of the apologist and martyr, St. Justin. St. Irenaeus, the first theologian to formulate the doctrine of image and likeness, quotes often from Justin. It is imperative, therefore, that the doctrine of the Logos, as the Image of the Father, be understood before we try to understand the doctrine of the Fathers concerning man's immanent relationship to Jesus Christ, the spoken Word Incarnate. Precisely from the traditional doctrine as handed down by St. Paul, St. John and St. Justin on the Divine Logos, the Greek Fathers would interpret Genesis 1. 26 as: "God created man to

His own Image that was the Interior Word existing from all eternity. Man is not created in the immediate image and likeness of God but according to the only Image and Likeness of God, that is, the Divine Logos, the Word that was made flesh."

SOURCE OF THE LOGOS DOCTRINE

The Fathers in speaking of the Divine Logos did not coin a new terminology. They found a rich doctrine already existing for centuries among the pagan philosophers and religious speculators. Divine writers of the Old and New Testaments were directly or indirectly influenced in their concept of the Logos by the Greek philosophies of Heraclitus and the Stoics and greatly by the religious speculation of Philo.

For the Greeks in general, Logos "means not only the side of God which is reflected in creation, which touches the finite world, it is the ultimate reason which explains all existence, the eternal principle that underlies phenomena."[6] Heraclitus (6th century, B.C.), with his theory of everything material and in flux, posited the Logos in all matter, giving to each being in its state of perpetual fluidity its order and regularity. It was the "rationale" behind the changes, the law of the world, criterion of truth, the rule of justice.

But the Stoics, in a reaction against Plato's dichotomy between the world of ideas separated from the material world of lesser reality, posited the Logos as Reason. Man participates in this Reason that is immersed in all being both as the interior Logos (*Logos endiathetos*) or Reason and as the externalized Logos (*Logos prosphorikos*),[7] the spoken word or reason expressed externally in activated speech.

Philo (died in 44 A.D.), the Alexandrian Jew

who tried to harmonize Hellenic Platonism with the revealed books of the Old Testament, made the Logos God's instrument of self-revelation whereby the inaccessible one God could make contact with the material world and man could be lifted into eternity.[8] Philo was aware of his incomplete concept of Logos, for he was taking as his foundation the Logos of God in the Old Testament, which under Hellenic influences was expressed ever more progressively as a separated, hypostatized creative principle that allowed the one God to retain His inaccessibility and independence while on the other hand there was established a communication through the Logos with God and creatures.

Logos becomes Wisdom personified in *Proverbs*, for example: "The Lord made me the beginning of His ways for His works. He established me before time was in the beginning before He made the earth . . . . I was by Him suiting myself to Him. I was that wherein He took delight."[9] From this influence and the speculation of Philo, St. John in the Prologue of his Gospel makes the Logos now clearly and indisputably a hypostatic Person, the second Person of the Blessed Trinity, the "Word abiding with Him and the Word was God. He abode, at the beginning of time, with God. It was through Him that all things came into being and without Him came nothing that has come to be . . . And the Word was made flesh and came to dwell among us."[10] St. John uses a concept of Logos already known to his Hellenic and Hebrew readers to make the ineffable mystery of the God-Man somewhat more intelligible. His Logos is now God, a Person, but still immanent in the world. With this brief sketch as background, we can turn to the first Christian philosopher, St. Justin, who prepared the way for Irenaeus and the other early theologians by his doctrine of Christ, the Logos, as Image of God.

GREEK PAIDEIA

Although Christianity sprang from within the Jewish community of Jerusalem, yet it developed an articulation of its fundamental truths in an environment predominantly Hellenistic in language, culture and philosophical thinking. Werner Jaeger has excellently outlined the dependency of early Christianity on the Greek paideia for its language medium, literary forms and philosophy.[11] This unhesitancy on the part of the early Christian thinkers to use the Hellenistic heritage as the ready-made medium for presenting Christianity to the cultured pagan and Jewish world of the 2nd and 3rd centuries was based on their deep belief in Christ, the Logos, already working before His incarnational appearance in flesh, among the pagans and the Old Testament Jews.

Much is being written today about "anonymous Christianity," in an attempt to show that all men have a positive relation to Christ's redemptive action and to His Church, even though they may not in fact be members of the visible Church. The non-Christian has from his first moment of creation been touched by the reality of Christ's redemptive work in his soul and in the universe which is the foundation of a positive orientation to the full Christian as found in Christ's visible Church. This was hardly new to the early Christian thinkers, especially to St. Justin who strove to point out apologetically the intimate relationship of pagan culture and the Old Testament to Christianity. In his *First Apology*, St. Justin describes the "anonymous Christians" of his times:

> Those who have lived according to *Reason* [the Greek word used by Justin is *Logos*] are Christians, even though accounted atheists. Such among the Greeks were Socrates and Heraclitus and others like

25

them; among the barbarians Abraham and Ananias and Azarias and Misael and Elias and many others, whose actions and names would, I know, be tedious to relate.[12]

It was the Logos who was revealing Himself to the pagan thinkers and inspiring them to write and do heroic things. In his *Second Apology*, Justin emphasizes the active role of the Divine Logos, Christ Himself, in the lives of the pre-Christian pagans:

For whatever either lawgivers or philosophers uttered well, they elaborated by finding and contemplating some part of the Word. But since they did not know the whole of the Word, which is Christ, they often contradicted themselves . . . . But in Christ, who was partially known even by Socrates (for He was and is the Word who is in every man, and who foretold the things that were to come to pass both through the prophets in His own Person when He was made of like passions, and taught these things), not only philosophers and scholars believed, but also artisans and people entirely uneducated, despising both glory and fear, and death, since He is a power of the ineffable Father and not the mere instrument of human reason.[13]

Thus, for Justin the pagan truth found in the Greek paideia was not complete but partial, yet not basically erroneous due to the presence of the Logos already actively working in space and time before He becomes flesh in the Incarnation. God was already communicating with the pagans, giving them and all men a certain content of revelation insofar as they opened themselves to the fulfillment of their human nature. Jean Danielou explains the relationship of God to man outside of His covenant of direct revelation by stating that, historically, man

26

belongs to the supernatural order. He does not oppose natural religion to supernatural religion in the sense that the first would be outside of the effective and concrete communication of God to man; but he feels, rather, it is natural in the sense of an action that takes place within the cosmos that is an attraction to consciousness wherein the One God is not only recognized but one lives according to this conviction. Thus this Cosmic Covenant, that Danielou applies to the pagans of pre-Christian times and those of the apologist Justin's epoch, is already a covenant of grace, differing from that of the New Covenant in its imperfect degree of God's self-revelation in the cosmos and its difficulty to be apprehended, due to frail humanity.[14]

LOGOS DOCTRINE OF JUSTIN

Justin speaks of the doctrine of Logos as a current notion, implying that it was more a traditional way of speaking of the role of Jesus Christ in the Trinity's activity towards the human race, than an esoteric manner of philosophizing about a Christian truth by using a concept already developed among pagans for centuries. We can safely say that he used the Logos doctrine in the light of what tradition believed was the role of Christ in the work of God.[15]

The first point fundamental for Justin in his apologetics with the Jews was to establish beyond doubt that the Logos was a Person, a truly substantial reality of the same nature yet numerically distinct from the Eternal Father. In several places in his *Dialogue with Trypho*, Justin stresses this:

But this Offspring, which was truly brought forth from the Father, was with the Father before all the creatures and the Father communed with Him; even as the Scripture by Solomon has made clear, that He whom Solomon calls Wisdom was begotten as a Beginning before all His creatures and as Offspring by God.[16]

Again, Justin emphasizes the distinctness of the Logos from the Father:

I shall endeavor to persuade you that He who is said to have appeared to Abraham and to Jacob and to Moses and who is called God is distinct from Him who made all things, numerically, I mean, not distinct in will. For I affirm that He has never at any time done anything which He who made the world—above whom there is no other God—has not wished Him both to do and to engage Himself with.[17]

The Logos is of the same nature as God, therefore He too is God and is to be worshipped equally. But as to the generation of this Divine Logos, clothed in mystery, Justin tries to give some understanding by way of analogies. All other beings are created works of God, but the Logos is His Child, His only Son, the unique, only Son.[18] God brings forth the Logos without any change or diminution.

He was begotten of the Father by an act of will; just as we see happening among ourselves; for when we bring forth some word, we beget the word which remains in us, when we give it out; and just as we see also happening in the case of fire, which is not lessened when it has kindled another but remains the same; that which has been kindled by it likewise appears to exist by itself, not diminishing that from which it was kindled.[19]

Justin has been accused of subordinationism. In his eagerness to present in an apologetic, understandable way the essential doctrine of the Christian faith, he tended to link up the generation of the Logos with the creation of the material world. The Logos doctrine held out an intrinsic attraction for the pagans schooled in Platonism. For them the Logos became easily the intermediate secondary diety, the *demiurgos*. For the Jews, the transcendence of God made the Logos equivalent to the Angel of Jahweh. In either case the consubstantiality of the Logos with the eternal Father was compromised. Johannes Quasten implies that Justin yielded to this danger of subordinationism in describing the relation between the Logos and the Father. Justin seems to suppose that the Logos became externally independent only in order to create and govern the world. This personal function or activity in the created order gave Him personal existence. He became a divine person but subordinated to the Father.[20]

However, Father Lagrange defends Justin's writings by attributing any apparent subordinationism to a faulty translation of the Greek text of Proverbs 8.22: "The Lord has formed me at the beginning of His ways, before His works . . ." This verse was inexactly translated as: "The Lord formed me *as* the beginning of His works." Father Lagrange argues that Justin could not forget the prologue of St. John: "In the beginning was the Word."[21] We also quoted earlier a text of Justin in which he clearly teaches the generation of the Logos before any creation.[22]

From Justin's doctrine of the Logos he drew two theological conclusions. The first is that God created all things in the cosmos through His Word, the Logos. He is far from the caution of Philo who, following his Neo-Platonic principles, posits the Logos as a mere exemplary cause, a model for material beings, but in no wise capable of making contact with sensible objects. The Logos, in His generation, comes from God with a relationship to the future created cosmos. This is the way God has decreed to create, "in and through the Logos."

This leads us to the second theological conclusion of Justin's doctrine, that of God's communication of Self through the Logos to mankind. Here again God so decrees freely to communicate with mankind through His Logos. Here Christ's own words come to mind: "No one knows the Son except the Father; nor does anyone know the Father except the Son and him to whom the Son chooses to reveal Him."[23] "No one has at any time seen God. The only begotten Son, Who is in the bosom of the Father, He has revealed Him."[24]

This Divine Logos, Jesus Christ, is the supreme event of God's infinite condescension to communicate Himself to mankind. Not only would He be the model, the Image of His Heavenly Father, according to which each individual man would be created, but He would actively effect, by the divine life of His Spirit dwelling in man through grace, that Image into its fullness, into the very Likeness of the Son of God Himself. With this as a background, we can turn now to the individual Greek Fathers and see how they developed the Image and Likeness doctrine.

CHAPTER THREE

ST. IRENAEUS

St. Irenaeus has justly been called the first Christian theologian. He was the first Christian writer to use the analogy of image and likeness as a theological framework around which he integrated an articulated teaching on grace, creation, anthropology, the psychology and asceticism of the entire spiritual life. He was born in Asia Minor near Smyrna between the years 140 and 160. As a boy he heard the Christian faith explained by Polycarp, bishop and martyr and disciple of the Beloved Disciple of the Lord, St. John the Evangelist. Eusebius records Irenaeus' letter to a Roman priest, Florinus, in which Irenaeus recalls how Polycarp:

> Reported his intercourse with John and with the others who had seen the Lord, how he remembered their words, and what were the things concerning the Lord which he had heard from them, and about their miracles and about their teachings and how Polycarp had received them from the eye-witnesses of the Word of Life and reported all things in agreement with the Scriptures. I listened eagerly even then to these things through the mercy of God which was given me, and made notes of them, not on paper, but in my heart, and ever by the grace of God do I truly ruminate on them.[1]

These words assure us, therefore, that Irenaeus was in touch with the apostolic tradition. But it is in his two main works that we realize how bent he was on remaining faithful to that tradition and to passing that teaching on. Irenaeus was primarily

31

a pastor of souls. Called from Asia Minor to Lyons in southern France for a reason unknown to us, he took over that church as bishop in 177 or 178. As bishop he felt his first duty was to protect his flock from the ravages of the spreading heresy of Gnosticism. From Irenaeus' work against Valentinus and the other Gnostics, *Adversus Haereses,* we can gather a fairly good idea of what 2nd century Gnosticism was like and why it posed a threat for the early Christian Church. This was basically an eclectic religious system mixed with theogony, cosmogony, world history, ascetical doctrine, philosophy and science. Christian truths and Scriptural citations were intermixed with gatherings from Persian and Egyptian cultic religions to create a hodgepodge of religious teaching.

Gnosticism, as Irenaeus outlines it in Book II of *Adversus Haereses* in his attempt to refute the gnostic system of the Valentinians and the Marcionites, sprang from a basic distrust of matter. This material world came about as a result of sin. In the beginning there were only spiritual beings called *eons* which lived in harmonious coordination according to various hierarchical degrees of perfection. One eon in dissension and rebellion broke off from this harmonious hierarchy to seek a place of higher perfection. The balance was disturbed and this eon was cast out. From this disarray of harmony sprang our universe, the work of a *demiurgos.* Yet divine sparks still inhabited the material creation of this universe. A savior-eon came down from heaven and took upon himself an apparent body in order to be like us and to gather up the divine sparks in us and lead us back to our origin. He accomplishes this by giving certain beings a hidden knowledge, a *gnosis,* which taught the saved souls the way back to heaven and provided the means of arriving there. God cannot have any part in our material creation: His transcendence is exaggerated to such an extent that He

32

becomes an abstraction accessible only through symbols intelligible only to the intellectually elite.

Thus man owes his material origin in this world to the demiurgos who creates three categories of human beings. The first class of men is made according to the image of God and are called *hylic* men.[2] These are pure and simple men who live completely according to their animal, materially corruptible natures. These men are not spiritual, hence will never reach immortality. With all matter they will perish by the fire that will come out of the center of the world. The Jews and pagans make up the majority of this class, who are content to live according to their material bodies and not according to the Spirit. The second class of men is called the *psychics*.[3] These possess sparks of immortality as well as materiality. They thus can opt for a higher category of being and reach salvation or turn to their lower selves and be destroyed along with all matter. These, the Gnostics claimed, were made to the likeness of God, yet were destined, even should they opt for the Spirit, to occupy an inferior rank of salvation. The third class, the esoteric group of *in-Gnostics* is called the *pneumatics*.[4] These are immortal and incorruptible by nature, and through the gnosis or secret knowledge given them by the Savior they will reach true salvation.

At the basis of this insidious doctrine of Gnosticism is a denial of the universal, salvific will of God towards all men. God apparently grants salvation to only a few chosen souls, those who by their nature have been made originally by God as spirits. Salvation is a re-divinization, a return to the full spiritual perfection in which these chosen souls were originally created. The rest of mankind, born not as pure spirits, but as participators in corruptible matter, could not have a chance for salvation. Again we see a basic erroneous tendency, common to Platonism, that matter is not only the source of evil and sin but is fundamentally evil in itself. Moral actions have no value in saving the *hylics* from corruption and final destruction. Man is really not free to accept God's freely offered gift of salvation. Man is predestined to a certain intellectual gnosis or lack thereof, over which state man has no control. Men are born in one of these three categories and no amount of moral effort can aid one in moving towards complete salvation. Jules Gross summarizes Gnosticism as less a crude Hellenization of Christianity and a more a superficial Christianization of a Hellenistic gnosis, clearly pagan and mystical in its exposition.[5]

Against this heresy of Gnosticism, proposed by Valentinus and Marcion especially, that postulated not God as Creator of the material world, but a *demiurgos*, and gave salvation according to an intellectual fatalism to those who happened to have been made pure spirits and hence inheritors of the hidden gnosis brought by the Savior-Logos, Irenaeus uses as a powerful instrument of teaching the true tradition, the doctrine of the image and likeness. He is not primarily interested in working out a complete doctrine acound the analogy of image and likeness. He is more concerned with the universality of God's salvific will and hence the unity of His divine, merciful condescensions throughout all the long history of His salvific communication with mankind. Hence Irenaeus lapses into an inconsistent use of these two terms, image and likeness, at times using them synonymously, but more often distinguishing them. His polemical purpose must be kept always in mind in an attempt to extricate a clear doctrine of Irenaeus concerning image and likeness.

IMAGE AND LIKENESS IN
FIRST CREATION

Irenaeus was the inheritor, along with the
Gnostics, of the Semitic emphasis on the transcendence and sovereignty of God. Yet Irenaeus recon-
ciles this transcendence of God and God's activity in
creation by turning to Holy Scripture and hearing
the words of God: "Let us make man in our image,
after our likeness" (Genesis, 1, 26). This is the
first step in the history of salvation of a long series
of salvific acts by God to bring man to his full end
in God. The first act of creation, as all others, was
done through the two hands of God, the Son and
the Holy Spirit. God retains always His preeminence
and sovereignty in the creation of man. God remains always the Uncreated Total Being, while
man remains always the imperfect, the dependent-
being-on-God. Clearly with the Gnostics in mind,
Irenaeus shows that God loses nothing of His power
or goodness in creating man, and man receives his
allness in the proportion that he submits to the active *hands* of God.

> With God there are simultaneously ex-
> hibited power, wisdom and goodness. His
> power and goodness appear in this, that
> of His own will He called into being and
> fashioned things having no previous ex-
> istence: His wisdom is shown in His hav-
> ing made created things parts of one har-
> monious and consistent whole; and those
> things which, through His super-eminent
> kindness, receive growth and a long period
> of existence, do reflect the glory of the
> uncreated One, of that God who bestows
> what is good ungrudgingly . . . And thus
> in all things God has the preeminence,
> who alone is uncreated, the first of all

things and the primary cause of the existence of all, while all other things remain under God's subjection. But being in subjection to God is continuance in immortality and immortality is the glory of the uncreated One. By this arrangement, therefore, and these harmonies and a sequence of this nature, man, a created and organized being, is rendered *according to the image and likeness of the uncreated God*—the Father planning everything well and giving His commands, the Son carrying these into execution and performing the work of creating and the Spirit nourishing and increasing what is made, but man making progress day by day and ascending towards the perfect, that is, approximating the uncreated One.[6]

In this text Irenaeus apparently refrains from distinguishing between the image and likeness,[7] for he is dealing with the first created man before the Fall. Man was destined to grow daily by his openness to the activities of God the Father unfolding His will in His providence and commands given to man, of the Son in carrying out these initial designs of the Father in created man and bringing man to his completion, and of the Holy Spirit in "nourishing and increasing" that divine life within man.

But in order to understand man, Irenaeus shows more specifically that Adam was created according to the image of Jesus Christ, the God-man. The Divine Logos made man was the pattern according to which God the Creator fashioned man. Jesus Christ is the Prototype of man; He is the man that Adam (and hence the whole human race) was destined to be in his fullness. In his *Proof of the Apostolic Preaching* Irenaeus makes this point:

'. . . for as the image of God did He make

man' (Gen. 9, 6) and the *image* is the Son of God in whose image man was made.[8]

The perfect image of God therefore is the Logos Incarnate. This image of Christ and of all *full* men possesses three necessary elements: body, soul and spirit:

> . . . there are three things out of which, as I have shown, the complete man is composed—flesh, soul and spirit.[9]

All three elements, as assumed by the humanity of Christ, are essential to man as God made him and intended him to be eventually completed. Against the Gnostics, for whom matter was the intrinsic principle of evil, Irenaeus strongly insists on the body as well as the soul as constituting man's image. Jesus Christ took on a body not only to redeem mankind but more precisely to be our perfect image or exemplar according to which all men, including those born before the Incarnation in time, were to be fashioned. Man is made not directly therefore to the image of God but according to the Image of God who is Jesus Christ. Thus Christ, taking upon Himself a human body and a human soul with intellect and will, manifested to us our true image.[10]

The body and soul form the *plasma* or the *frame* of man. This is his image. Yet he needs the *spirit* to complete his being, just as the perfect man, Jesus Christ, our Image, was completed by the Spirit. In the following citation we see Irenaeus' clear distinction between image and likeness, as corresponding to: image=body and soul; likeness=spirit or the life of God (grace) dwelling in the total man, body and soul. Commentators have used this and similar texts to show that Irenaeus distinguishes clearly between the natural and supernatural. But distinction was not separateness for Irenaeus, who viewed the spirit as a drawing out through the operations of the Holy Spirit of the powers placed in man's image by the Creator. Man as mere body and soul, according to Irenaeus, is imperfect as a total man. Hence, though he clearly admits that the likeness may be acquired and again may be lost, admitting therefore of a progressive growth to a point of full perfection, spirit is a necessary component of the full and perfect man as it was in the perfect Prototype for all men, Jesus Christ. This becomes clear from Irenaeus' text:

> Now the soul and the spirit are certainly a part of the man but certainly not the man; for the perfect man consists in the commingling and the union of the soul receiving the spirit of the Father and the admixture of that fleshly nature, which was moulded after the image of God. . . . But when the spirit here blended with the soul is united to God's handiwork (plasma), the man is rendered spiritual and perfect because of the outpouring of the Spirit, and this is he who was made in the image and likeness of God. But if the Spirit be wanting to the soul, he who is such is indeed of an animal nature, and, being left carnal, shall be an imperfect being, possessing indeed the image of God in his formation (in plasmate), but not receiving the similitude through the Spirit, and thus is this being imperfect . . . . Neither is the soul itself, considered apart by itself, the man; but it is the soul of a man, and part of a man. Neither is the spirit a man, for it is called the spirit, and not a man; but the commingling and union of all these constitutes the perfect man . . . . For this cause he (Paul) declares that those are 'the perfect' who present unto the Lord the three component parts without offence. Those then are

the perfect who have had the Spirit of God remaining in them, and have preserved their souls and bodies blameless, holding fast the faith of God, that is, that faith which is directed towards God and maintaining righteous dealings with respect to their neighbors.[11]

PARADISE LOST

Adam was born an image of the Image, Jesus Christ, in possessing a human, material body and a soul with the knowing and willing faculties that allowed him to know God and His will and love Him by obeying. The likeness that he possessed was the Divine Life possessed in an embryonic form, susceptible to increasing growth as the first man cooperated with the two hands of God, the Logos and the Holy Spirit, in doing the will of the Creator. He was a child (*pais* in Greek) as far as this Divine Life was developed. He was destined to move to greater maturity, to spiritual adulthood as he cooperated with the Divine Energies working in his person, not in his soul nor in his body as in distinct and separated parts, but in these essential, component parts making up a total personal being.

It is the Holy Spirit that gives man the gift of spiritual child-likeness; that is, that makes him a child to the likeness of the natural Son of God, the Logos, who is not only the model and exemplar of man's image but also of his likeness.[12] Jesus Christ sends His Holy Spirit to make man into a child of God. But this child has meaning only in reference to the goal, the adult man, the full son of God by participation (2 Peter, 1, 4). God gives His Holy Spirit through the Logos in an act of continued creation through greater growth in the spirit.

For as God is always the same, so also man,

39

when found in God, shall always go on towards God. For neither does God at any time cease to confer benefits upon or to enrich man; nor does man ever cease from receiving the benefits and being enriched by God. For the receptacle of His goodness and the instrument of His glorification is the man who is grateful to Him that made him.[13]

But when Adam sinned, he lost the spirit and hence he lost the likeness to God. To describe the Divine Life in man, Irenaeus very frequently uses the synonym *aptharsia* (incorruptibility) or *agennesia* (uncreatedness) for only God or one who shares in His divinity can be incorruptible and participate in the fullness of being, which means uncreatedness.

By their continuing in being throughout a long course of ages, they (men) shall receive a faculty of the Uncreated, through the gratuitous bestowal of eternal existence upon them by God . . . . But being in subjection to God is continuance in immortality and immortality is the glory of the Uncreated One. By this arrangement, therefore and these harmonies and a sequence of this nature, man, a created and organized being, is rendered after the image and likeness of the Uncreated God.[14]

God alone is incorruptible and uncreated. Man, through the gift of Divine Life, possesses the childhood that will mature into an unending, eternal adulthood of participated divinity that for Irenaeus was best described by the attributes of God as incorruptible and uncreated. But Adam lost this gift of Life and, though he possessed his human physical life, he became *corruptible* and *dead* as far as God's life within him was concerned. The likeness to God was extinguished although the image—body and soul — remained which possessed within it the seeds for man's rebirth into a refound likeness.

Yet the Devil, the Prince of Death, held man in his power. Adam failed to turn within himself and did not listen to the Word of God telling him of the Heavenly Father. Adam failed to cooperate with the Holy Spirit who was nourishing the divine childlikeness in man to its fullness. In a beautiful passage Irenaeus shows that man's fall was not because God loved less; man alone was at fault.

> How then shall he be a God who has not as yet been made a man? Or how can he be perfect who was but lately created? How again can he be immortal who in his mortal nature did not obey his Maker? . . . . If however thou wilt not believe in Him and wilt flee from His hands, the cause of imperfection shall be in thee who didst not obey, but not in Him who called thee . . . . The skill of God therefore is not defective, for He has power of the stones to raise up children for Abraham; but the man, who does not obtain it, is the cause to himself of his own imperfection. The light does not fail because some persons have become blind. The light remains ever the same. It is those who are blinded that are involved in darkness through their own fault. The light does not enslave anyone by necessity; nor does God exercise compulsion upon anyone unwilling to accept the exercise of His skill. Those persons, therefore, who have apostatized from the light given by the Father and transgressed the law of liberty have done so through their own fault since they have been created free agents and possessed of power over themselves.[15]

For Irenaeus to truly live is to be united with

God; to separate from God is death. It is to leave
the light for darkness; to abandon order for chaos.
Man's only hope lay in ANOTHER greater than
man and the Devil, one who could regain for man
this lost life, this likeness to God.

PARADISE REGAINED

To express Christ's role in restoring the *spirit*
to man, Irenaeus uses the word *anakephalaiosis*
(recapitulation) which he borrows from Justin and
St. Paul.

> In his book against Marcion, Justin well
> says: "I would not have believed the Lord
> Himself, if He had announced any other
> than He who is our framer, maker and
> nourisher. But because the only-begotten
> Son came to us from the 'One God who both
> made this world and formed us and con-
> tains and administers all things, summing
> up His own handiwork in Himself, my
> faith towards Him is steadfast and my love
> to the Father immoveable, God bestowing
> both upon us.[16]

This "summing up His own handiwork in Himself" is Justin's paraphrase of St. Paul's passage in
Ephesians:

> And this good pleasure He decreed to put
> into effect in Christ when the designated
> period of time had elapsed, namely, to
> gather all creation both in heaven and on
> earth under one head, Christ (*anakephal-
> aiosasthai*).[17]

Irenaeus himself gives in the first book of his
theological synthesis, *Against Heresies*, his interpretation of Paul's passage:

> . . . the beloved Christ Jesus, our Lord, . . .
> (will) 'gather all things in one' (Eph. 1,

10) and (will) raise up anew all flesh . . .
and that He should execute just judgment
towards all; that He may send 'spiritual
wickednesses' (Eph. 6, 12) and the angels
who transgressed and became apostates,
together with the ungodly and the unright-
eous and wicked and profane among men,
into everlasting fire; but may, in the exercise of His grace, confer immortality on
the righteous and holy and those who have
kept His commandments . . . and may sur-
round them with everlasting glory.[18]

In an even more conclusive text Irenaeus shows
the recapitulation of Christ as He restores on every
level and stage of life our communion with God:

For in what way could we be partakers of
the adoption of sons, unless we had received
from Him through the Son that fellowship
which refers to Himself, unless His Word,
having been made flesh, had entered into
communion with us? Wherefore also He
passed through every stage of life, restoring to all communion with God . . . . But
what He did appear, that He also was: God
recapitulated in Himself the ancient formation of man, that He might kill sin, deprive death of its power and vivify man;
and therefore His works are true.[19]

Here we see, in St. Irenaeus' Pauline usage of
the symbol of recapitulation and of image and likeness, examples of patristic connotative language
rich with deep insights for us who have generally
lost this way of habitually thinking. The theory
of recapitulation stands at the center of Irenaeus'
theological system and describes best the role of
Jesus Christ in His Incarnation. It connotes a re-
beginning of the human race, now, however, back
in the opposite direction where Adam originally
found himself upon his creation. Christ reverses the

process that hurtled sin-infected man and the entire cosmos that was under his dominion away from true Light, Life and Incorruption towards sin, chaos and death. God gathers up again in His Logos His entire work by fulfilling it according to His original plan through an intimate association with the living Logos in the individual human being, made according to this Image and Likeness of God that is Christ.

This term, *recapitulation*, therefore, as Emile Mersch explains,[20] can refer to a resume, a taking up of all since the beginning, a recommencement, a return to the source, a restoration, a reorganization and incorporation under one Head. Irenaeus time and again teaches that in His work of recapitulation Christ went through all of the experiences of Adam but with total success. Christ does not merely undo, detail by detail, all that Adam had done to get mankind into its chaotic state. Christ's restoration of man (and with him as the center of this created cosmos of the whole material universe) is a dynamic process of growth and conflict. Christ is the Champion of the human race who enters into the battle to overcome the Evil One.[21] But Christ's work is not merely returning creation to its pristine state before the fall. To the concept of restoration, Irenaeus adds that of completion through a process of development in growth, as we have already seen in God's original plan before the Fall, from an embryonic life, through childhood, finally arriving at full manhood of the Divine Life. To show how Christ effected the restoration of man, Irenaeus uses exact analogies between the activities of Christ and those of Adam.[22] Here we see Irenaeus' existential approach to Christ's redemptive action as touching not only the Incarnation and the Cross but every action of His human life with redemptive significance.

But Christ's activities are not mere mechanical reduplications of the actions of Adam through perfect obedience to His Heavenly Father, whereby Christ undoes the disobedience of Adam. Satan is overthrown, the cosmos is removed from death's power. Yet this does not complete Christ's work of recapitulation since it does not fulfill the created plan of God. Christ's activities, through the agency of His divinely instituted Church with its divinely commissioned authority to teach His living word and to administer His sacraments, are still prolonged in the universe. Christ is still dynamically inserted through His glorious resurrected life into our universe. It is the Church that provides the *locus* of man's encounter with Christ the Fulfiller. Through the Church Christ gives man back again the Divine Life lost through sin. The likeness of Christ in Adam was lost through sin but restored in individual men through Christ's salvific actions in His Church.

A text of Irenaeus that had perhaps more influence on later patristic writers than any other text from the early Fathers explains in summary fashion the purpose of the Incarnation of the Word. Origen, Athanasius and all the succeeding Eastern Fathers would repeat this text:

> For this is why the Word of God is man, and this is why the Son of God became the Son of Man, that man might possess the Word, receive adoption and become the son of God. In no other way could we receive incorruptibility and immortality except by being united with incorruptibility and immortality. But how could we be united with incorruptibility and immortality, unless incorruptibility and immortality had first become what we are, in order that what is corruptible might be absorbed by incorruptibility and what is mortal by immortality, that so we might receive the adoption of sons?[23]

The Divine Word, becoming man, brought to

mankind the possibility of a new creation unto a new life. This new creation did not dissolve the other nor did it destroy it. It builds upon the physical, the natural, transforming it into a new life that makes man truly according to the likeness of God.

> What, then, did the Lord bring at His coming? Know that He brought all newness, by bringing Himself, who had been foretold. For this was announced, that a Newness would come, to renew and give life to man.[24]

Jesus Christ brings us this new life. Often St. Ireneaus speaks about the Spirit of Christ or the Holy Spirit as the principle and source of this Divine Life in us. It is this Holy Spirit that Christ brings us "who purifies man and raises him up to the life of God."[25] This "life of God" is a purely gratuitous gift from God distinct from man's natural life. Here we see a clear distinction in Irenaeus' thinking, although he does not wish to separate nature from grace.

> He (the Spirit) speaks respecting the salvation of man: 'He asked life of Thee and Thou gavest him length of days for ever and ever,' (Ps. 21,4) indicating that it is the Father of all who imparts continuance for ever and ever on those who are saved. For life does not arise from us, nor from our own nature; but it is bestowed according to the grace of God. And therefore he who shall preserve the life bestowed upon him and give thanks to Him who imparted it, shall receive also length of days for ever and ever.[26]

Congar points out quite aptly that in the mind of Irenaeus these two orders were distinct but in continuity one with the other. "Nature appears as an imperfect participation of God of which grace realizes perfectly the likeness but in the same line."[27] Irenaeus seeks various analogies to show the continuity between nature and grace, natural life and the life of the Spirit, between image and likeness. His favorite is that of the engrafted wild olive tree. We in our natural life, the image of Christ, that was made by God to bear fruit by being inserted into the Divine Life, do not lose our nature through the infusion of divine grace, but to it is given a new force, a new power to enable it to bring forth fruit of a totally different nature.

> But as the engrafted wild olive does not certainly lose the substance of its wood, but changes the quality of its fruit and receives another name, being now not a wild olive, but a fruit-bearing olive and is called so, so also when man is grafted in by faith and receives the Spirit of God, he certainly does not lose the substance of flesh, but changes the quality of the fruit of his works and receives another name, showing that he has become changed for the better, being now not mere flesh and blood but a spiritual man and is called such.[28]

Again, Irenaeus distinguishes between the "breath of life which renders man an animated being" and the "vivifying Spirit which causes him to become spiritual."[29] Irenaeus uses the various examples from the life of Our Lord of miraculous cures ending up with the resurrection of Lazarus from the dead to life to illustrate this new life given by the Holy Spirit.[30]

The important question to be asked at this point is whether Irenaeus recognized a real distinction between the Holy Spirit as Giver and the "likeness" of God in man as the gift? In terms familiar to Western theologians, did Irenaeus admit a real distinction between the uncreated Energy, the Holy Spirit, working within man to effect his sanctification and the created energy or created grace that as an accident to man's nature admits of progression in growth? Clearly and in many texts Irenaeus distinguishes between the Holy Spirit and the effect He works in man. It is the Holy Spirit that "has formed man to the likeness of God."[31] The likeness of God in man consists not only of God's Divine Life in a participated manner but consists also of other supernatural gifts. Two such gifts distinct from the Giver are incorruptibility and immortality, associated with the broader categories of life and communion. This was, as has been already pointed out, the raison d'etre of Christ's incarnation, "to abolish death and bring to light life and bring about communion of God and man."[32] Through the Son, the Holy Spirit "in the end of times has been poured forth in a new manner upon humanity over all the earth renewing man to God."[33] It was the Holy Spirit that rendered man immortal, referring not to the philosophical notion of immortality of the soul, but to an added gift whereby man even in this life began to live the life of God within himself.

Without saying it in our terms of grace, Irenaeus insists again and again on the same doctrine that we understand by the terms uncreated and created grace.[34] The Holy Spirit is possessed by man and His energizing activity brings about as effect, distinct from Himself, the Cause, a created grace or gift that renders man more and more *like* to God.[35] This created gift transfigures man more and more into an adopted son of God.[36] Yet this created gift can be lost again by man, in closing his ears to God's communications and thus he becomes as the first Adam, dead to the true life.

> It is good to obey God and to believe in Him and keep His commandments and this is life for man. Not to obey God is evil and this is man's death.[37]

But both the uncreated Grace that is the Holy Trinity itself in its condescending, merciful love for man and the created grace that is the degree of likeness of man to God, along with the gifts of enlightenment to the intellect and strength given to the will to live according to the new dignity of a son of God, are not viewed by Irenaeus as static gifts, present within man but exercising no change in man's nature. Again recalling the simple analogy of the wild olive tree inserted into a fruit-bearing tree that Irenaeus uses, we can see that he is concerned to present the relationship of the new life (spirit-created likeness of God in man) of the Spirit (uncreated Life of God) to man's human nature (body and soul-created image of Christ in man) in the setting of a dynamic growth process.

God's presence and our divinization into God's likeness call out for activity, first on the part of the Trinity to work within us through the conflicts of every moment as Providence manifests God's holy will-in-action, and secondly on the part of us transformed into true sons of God by participation. Our activity is to be a response in increased faith, hope and charity towards the immanent God within us. In a *synergism* man cooperates with God in his activities to aid this growth in the three virtues that are unitive habits with the Divine Indwelling Trinity. The sacraments also are, besides the daily activities, the points of encountering Divinity in order to be nourished anew in God's life.

It is especially in conflict and suffering. Irenaeus tells us, that God sends us the means to purify ourselves of *unrighteousness*, that is, any obstacle to the growth of righteousness, the term St. Irenaeus often uses to mean the Divine Life within man. In a passage that shows well how the presence in man of the two hands of the Father, the Logos and the Holy Spirit, works to bring about a more vibrant image and likeness in man, we see also man's self-activity:

> And therefore throughout all time, man, having been moulded at the beginning by the hands of God, that is, of the Son and of the Spirit, is made after the image and likeness of God: the chaff, indeed, which is the apostasy, being cast away; but the wheat, that is, those who bring forth fruit to God in faith, being gathered into the barn. And for this cause tribulation is necessary for those who are saved, that having been after a manner broken up, and rendered fine, and sprinkled over by the patience of the Word of God, and set on fire (for purification), they may be fitted for the royal banquet. As a certain man of ours said, when he was condemned to the wild beasts because of his testimony with respect to God: 'I am the wheat of Christ and am ground by the teeth of the wild beasts, that I may be found the pure bread of God.'[38]

But during this life-time man is always in the process of growing to spiritual adulthood. It is only in the life to come that man will reach the goal of all his striving and all the concerted activities over his whole lifetime by the Divine Energies dwelling within man. God's initial creation will not be annihilated but only its modality of material existence will cease to be; "For neither is the substance nor the essence of creatures annihilated . . . but 'the fashion of the world passes away.'" (I Cor. 7, 31)[39] Man will live renewed in this incorruptible state,

> . . . so as to preclude the possibility of becoming old. Then there shall be the new heaven and the new earth in which man

shall continually remain, always holding fresh converse with God.[40]

Irenaeus ends his monumental work, *Against Heresies*, by a statement that sums up well his basic orientation throughout the entire work. Then in the beatific vision the saved will contemplate God and all creatures in Him; yet the mysteries of His great love for mankind will never be understood by man.

> For there is the one Son, who accomplished His Father's will; and one human race also in which the mysteries of God are wrought, 'which the angels desire to look into' (I Pet. 1, 12) and they are not able to search out the wisdom of God by means of which His handiwork, confirmed and incorporated with His Son, is brought to perfection; that His offspring, the First-begotten Word should descend to the creature, that is, to what had been moulded (plasma) and that it should be contained by Him; and, on the other hand, the creature should contain the Word and ascend to Him, passing beyond the angels and be made after the image and likeness of God.[41]

CHAPTER FOUR
CLEMENT OF ALEXANDRIA

Clement's personality and approach to Christianity would meet with a sympathetic response today among modern Christians. Born a pagan with an opportunity to deepen his Hellenic studies by travel, this Christian convert was attracted to all types of philosophies and natural theologies as containing some *natural* revelation made by God to searching man outside of the Judaeo-Greco revelation. Above all, the beauties of pagan Hellenic culture attracted him. He writes in his *Paedogogos*:

> Why should I not enjoy them? For whom
> have they been created if not for us?[1]

And again in a similar vein he writes in his *Stromata*:

> One true God is the sole author of all
> beauty, whether it is Hellenic or whether
> it is ours.[2]

His attitude towards the prevalent philosophies of his times, Platonism, Stoicism and the eclectic Gnosticism, is decidedly different from that of Irenaeus and the earlier apologists except perhaps for Justin. Clement does not negatively reject Gnosticism nor does he oppose it polemically with a barrage of arguments that call more to faith in tradition rather than a rational process of probing to understand the good contained in the opposite views.

Error is never for Clement one hundred percent opposed to truth existing in a pure, distilled state. Error exists in individuals who possess the truth but in an embryonic, often very primitive form, needing to be complemented and fulfilled. Clement is in constant *dialogue* with the world in which he lives. His optimism towards it, its institutions and men, in particular, stems primarily from his

52

basic belief in the unity of all human history as rooted in and permeated by the Logos, the Second Person of the Trinity, Jesus Christ. All human history, whether pagan, Old Testament or New, has its significance in and through Christ. Christ is the Divine Pedagogue, sent by His Father to teach us the perfect way back to Heaven.

His theology, therefore, is primarily an incarnational one. He does not deny the value of Christ's redemptive act in His sacrifice on the Cross nor its reality in the Mass. Clement's main writings that we possess give us a different point of emphasis determined from the intention and audience that he had in mind when he wrote them. He is fundamentally a Christian teacher, teaching all truth-seeking men. Like Socrates, Clement avoided any systematic organization through which he taught his disciples. He taught by stirring up questions in the minds of his listeners. Truth was not taught so much as it was *encountered*. A good teacher only prepared the environment for this encountering event with truth.

All persons of whatever religious or philosophical beliefs were welcomed by Clement to hear his message. He unfolds his *weltanschauung* in terms of the Gnostic divisions of human beings that were well known to his listeners. We have already presented these in dealing with Irenaeus' approach to the Gnostics of his time. Men, according to the Gnostics, are divided into three divisions. The *hylics* (*hylikoi*) were completely dominated by matter and hence were predestined to annihilation along with matter. The *pneumatics* (*pneumatikoi*) were born spiritual beings, given by birth a *gnosis* or knowledge of a hidden revelation that predestined them to be saved. The *psychics* (*psychikoi*) were in between these two predetermined groups and had the possibility of opting for the superior or inferior category.

Clement uses this basic division but gives it a complete Christian orientation. His fundamental stress is placed on the universal will of God to save all men; hence Clement highlights the possibility of all men being saved, provided man with his free will consents to cooperate with God's condescending will-act towards all men.

Struck by the unity rather than the disparity separating divisions of men, Clement uses these three basic categories in such a way as to insure the universal salvific will of God and man's freedom. The *hylics*, for Clement, are the pagans, living a natural, material existence, vaguely aware of a higher supernatural order. Yet they are being called by God constantly to embrace the higher realms of the really real. The *psychics* are the Christians of simple faith, those who are still immersed in a material approach to God; those who take the Holy Scriptures literally and cannot see beyond the letter of the word. The *pneumatics* are the Christian Gnostics who, through their cooperation by a lifetime of ascetical purification, reach an interior *gnosis* or knowledge of God and the spiritual world hidden behind the material appearances of the *phenomenal* world.

It is this Christian Gnosticism that we must keep in mind in exploring Clement's doctrine of the image and likeness. It seems that his three main writings were written as a trilogy following this gnostic division. His first main work, the *Protrepticos* or *Exhortation to the Greeks*, was addressed to the heathens, the *hylics*. His second work, the *Paedagogos* or *Tutor*, is addressed as the second step in a unified progression from faith to vision. It is directed to Christians in general in order to exhort them to higher perfection in imitation of the Divine Teacher. The last, the *Stromata* or *Miscellanies* is not an organized, logical work but seeks to comment in a spirit of utter freedom with no systematization on a variety of often unrelated topics.

J. Quasten claims that Clement had intended the third book of the trilogy to be called the *Didaskalos* or *Teacher*, which would have been directed towards the *pneumatics* or Gnostic Christians.[3] Clement probably saw that the topic was such that neither a book nor his talents in organizing such a delicate synthesis could produce the effect he desired. Much, therefore, that Clement says about the spiritual progression of man from a son of God in potency to the actual fullness in the eternal life is expressed in terms of a theology of *gnosis* or knowledge.

One of Clement's important contributions is his constant stress on the continuity of man's nature and his supernatural destiny. Thus in dealing with the concept of image and likeness of God in man, Clement, unlike Irenaeus, does not distinguish clearly between a state of natural affinity to the Logos by reason of the body and soul (the image) and a state of supernatural kinship to the Trinitarian Life (the likeness). Clement describes man in his relationship to God:

'For God created man for immortality and made him an image of His own nature' (Wisdom 2, 25), according to which nature of Him who knows all, he who is a Gnostic and righteous and holy with prudence, hastens to reach the measure of perfect manhood.[4]

This being called man is created to become immortal, to live forever. His destiny is to give glory to God by "containing the Lord." In a beautiful passage in his *Protrepticos*, Clement compares man to a harp, a pipe and a temple:

And he who is of David, and yet before him, the Word of God, despising the lyre and harp which are but lifeless instruments, and having tuned by the Holy Spirit the universe, and especially man . . . makes melody to God of this instrument of many tones; and to this instrument—I mean—he sings accordant: 'For thou art my harp, and pipe and temple'[5]—a harp for harmony—a pipe by reason of the Spirit—a temple by reason of the word; so that the first may sound, the second breathe, the third contain the Lord.[6]

And again, he says:

A beautiful breathing instrument of music the Lord made man, after His image.[7]

But Clement cannot remain long before he returns to the Logos. Following in the tradition of Irenaeus he distinguishes that Jesus Christ is the true Image of God and true man is the image of the Image, Christ, insofar as man puts on the mind of Christ:

For the image of God is His Word, the genuine Son of Mind, the Divine Word, the archetypal light of light; and the image of the Word is the true man, the mind which is in man, who is therefore said to have been made 'in the image and likeness of God,'' assimilated to the Divine Word in the affections of the soul and therefore rational.[8]

Man is different from all other creatures on the earth because man alone through his intellectual capacity and proper use of it has been constituted by nature for fellowship and communal existence with God.

For man has been otherwise constituted by nature, so as to have fellowship with God . . . . So placing our finger on what is man's peculiar and distinguishing characteristic above other creatures, we invite him—born, as he is, for the contemplation of heaven and being, as he is a truly heavenly plant—to the knowledge of God counselling him to furnish himself with what is his sufficient provision for eternity, namely piety.[9]

Contrary to Irenaeus' polemical insistence against the Gnostics who denied that the image of God was also to be found in the man's material body, Clement, using a basic Platonic principle, holds that man in his most distinguishing characteristic as man and the possessor of future eternal life reflects the image of God insofar as he possesses a mind (*nous*).

> For conformity with the image and likeness is not meant of the body (for it were wrong for what is mortal to be made like what is immortal), but in mind and reason, on which fitly the Lord impresses the seal of likeness, both in respect of doing good and of exercising rule.[10]

Again more clearly, Clement links up the Divine Logos as the Image of God, and man in his mind is made as image to the Image since, having an intellect and will, man can imitate the Logos and be assimiliated to Him.

> For the image of God is the divine and royal Word, the impassible man; and the image of the image is the human mind. And if you wish to apprehend the likeness by another name, you will find it named in Moses, a divine correspondence.[11]

Clement shows in one text that he is aware of the distinction between image and likeness but he rarely uses it, perhaps as has been said, because of his emphasis on the unity of man's progressive assimilation to God.

> For is it not thus that some of our writers have understood that man straightway on his creation received what is 'according to the image', but that what is according 'to

the likeness' he will receive afterwards on his perfection?[12]

But man's assimilation to God was to be brought about by man's free cooperation. Adam was to grow in virtue and thus grow into a likeness with God. Salvation was not a predestination given by God to a few chosen Gnostics without any effort on their part, but God wishes to save man through man's efforts. The heretics (Gnostics) proposed the dilemma concerning Adam's creation. If Adam were created perfect, how could he have sinned? If he were created imperfect, then God's creation would have been imperfect. To this Clement proposes an answer that in substance shows us the same distinction between image and likeness as proposed by Irenaeus. Yet in a more subtle way, he keeps contact with the Gnostics of his time by deemphasizing the distinctness by stressing the continuity in progressive growth.

> Adam was not perfect in his creation, but adapted to the reception of virtue. For it is of great importance in regard to virtue to be made fit for its attainment. And it is intended that we should be saved by ourselves. This, then, is the nature of the soul, to move itself. . . . Now an aptitude is a movement towards virtue . . . .[13]

Adam was to progress in virtue, which brought him to a greater likeness of God. Yet Adam turned from the path of virtue and he exchanged an immortal life for our mortal existence. He "neglected what is true and good on which account he exchanged his immortal life for a mortal life."[14] Adam's sin affected the whole human race of which he was the father by bequeathing to men a proclivity to sin along with a darkening of the intellect through ignorance.[15]

THE ROLE OF THE LOGOS

Irenaeus gave us a well-worked out Christology, following the traditional teaching of the Church of his times. Clement, although not against the traditional teaching of the Church concerning Christ, was a teacher, stirring up new insights by melding the traditional Christianity and Hellenic philosophy. Clement starts with his theory of the Cosmic Logos. His famed disciple, Origen, and the Alexandrian school after him would follow Clement on this central outlook. The historical appearance of Christ is important, but it is for Clement only one of many Logos manifestations among men. Irenaeus made the historical Incarnation the central point of all human history. Clement approaches the historical Christ from a detached philosophical viewpoint as a person that manifests certain abiding principles during His lifetime, which also were manifested in varying degrees in the Logos' appearance in the creation of the world and in Old Testament history as well as in His active manifestation among the pagans of old. What is of prime importance for Clement is not the details of these manifestations but the permanent, continuing principles cloaked in the historical appearances of the Logos. Whether the Logos was being manifested through the philosophers of old, the Old Testament prophets, in the humanity of the historical Jesus Christ or in the Church, the important point for Clement is not the event but the *principle* of divine action that the Logos is revealing to men.

The constantly recurring principle in all of the theophanies of the Logos is that which Clement expresses as the purpose of the Incarnation. Here we see the influence of St. Irenaeus' recapitulation theory on Clement:

> . . . the Word of God became man, that

thou mayest learn from man how man may become God.[16]

He insists on the absolute necessity of the Word Incarnate to restore us to immortality and to life. But when Clement descends to greater details as to the purpose of the Incarnation, he sees this again in line with the other manifestations in history of the Logos, namely, to reveal to mankind the interior mind of God the Father. Christ's essential work consists in illuminating the darkened minds of men. The Logos is an instructor and teacher sent by the Father to teach men the necessary knowledge of God that, when attained, divinizes. The knowing subject, as Plato had taught in the *Thetetes*,[17] "became assimilated as far as possible to God," the known object. For Clement, it is by learning from the revealing, divine Teacher, Jesus Christ, that man is divinized.

CHRISTIAN GNOSTICISM

Clement, although he does not work out an entire theology of man's divinization whereby he moves progressively closer to God Himself, yet he does open up some very interesting avenues of speculation on Christ's role as our illuminator and our salvation conceived as a *gnosis*.

The Christianity, however, that Clement presents to us is hardly pure *intellectualism*. He is as much a realist as an optimist, keenly aware of the obstacles that our fallen human natures place in the path of knowing and hence loving God more perfectly. And for this reason he dwells much on the necessity of man's efforts toward purification leading to a *katharsis* that in its final stages brought with it *apatheia*, that state of complete reintegration of all sense and psychic life with an intellect and will informed by God's own life (grace). He outlines the necessary virtues that would eliminate sin and lead to *apathy (apatheia)*. But it is his doctrine of *apatheia* that would be taken up by the monks of the desert through the formulation of Evagrius of Pontus,[18] John Climacus[19] and the entire Byzantine Hesychastic school of spirituality. It would become the external criterion or measure of one's growth in divine likeness. Clement goes much farther in his doctrine of *apatheia*, namely, of actually stamping out passions so that they no longer exist for the *passionless* man.[20] Here we see Clement clearly carried away by Stoic influence which led him to make many contradictory remarks about the role of the passions in man for good or evil.

In several passages Clement intimately connects man's degree of attained *apatheia* with the degree of the likeness of God in him. When a man has attained *gnosis* and lives always according to divine love, his passions (meaning the disordered element in man) dry up and die away.

> For by going away to the Lord, for the love he bears Him, . . . he does not withdraw himself from life . . . But he has withdrawn his soul from the passions . . . And on the other hand he lives, having put to death his lusts, and no longer makes use of the body, but allows it the use of necessaries that he may not give cause for dissolution.[21]

The passionless man, Clement continues, has no more need of fortitude for he is no more surrounded by dangers who possesses the object of his love.[22] No longer is there need for self-restraint for to have such desires that need self-restraint is "characteristic of one who is not yet pure, but subject to passion."[23]

But he seems aware also that *apatheia* is a mere condition for the more positive effect of acting reflectively and consciously as befits a divinized son of God. To describe the end of man's likeness to God, he moves it away from the danger of becoming a mere moral resemblance and considers it as a truly ontological state which he calls *theopoiesis* (divinization).

Although the word *theopoiein* (to divinize) was commonly used in the pagan classical and Hellenic literature to signify a divinization by *association*[24] it was Clement, as Jules Gross points out, who first among the early Christian writers commonly used this unbiblical term to express a most biblical concept, namely, that the Trinitarian life within man through grace truly divinizes man's nature making man a true son of God by adoption. After Clement, this very concept and its substantive, *theopoiesis*, would be commonly used by all the Greek Fathers.[25]

To reach this stage of divinization which is synonymous with the stage of *gnosis*, Clement again returns to his Gnostic categories of men to describe the role of the Logos. The hylics or pagans were given an illumination by the Logos to pass from their paganism to embrace the Christian faith. Clement then distinguishes among Christians a double faith. The *common* faith of the mass of Christians knows God and accepts the truths revealed by Him and "do not practice any injustice."[26] This is the faith of the *psychi*.

But there is a more perfect faith, that of the *pneumatics* or *Gnostics*. This is a deeper, more penetrating faith that Clement in the first chapter of Book V of his *Stromata* likens to the gift of hearing. The Gnostic possessing this inner faith is able to pierce through the *ta onta* (the things perceived by the senses) to arrive at the *noeta* (the intelligible quality that gives the true essence of any given being). This is the only full, perfect Christian. To possess this faith is the goal towards which all Christians should strive, but it will be attained in its perfection only after the last resurrection.[27] J.

Lebreton describes in a synthetic way Clement's Christian Gnostic:

> The Gnostic possesses science and perfect virtue, he knows all, attains all, comprehends all; each action is rectitude itself. No more passions exist; transfigured in God the Gnostic prays to Him without ceasing, his life is a perpetual feast. He is an apostle, priest. He constitutes not only an elite but a veritable heirarchy of the Church.[28]

We see in Clement's characterization of the Gnostic the basic outline of the spiritual life that Origen inherited from Clement and then passed on to Evagrius. The first level in the ascent to the *gnosis* is the purification that is brought about by *praxis* or the practice of virtuous, mortifying actions. Such virtues developed *apatheia*, which prepared the ground for an infusion of deeper faith, leading the Christian to *theoria* or contemplation, another name that Clement often uses for *gnosis*.[29] Contemplation he divides into two levels of infused gifts by God. The first, *theoria practica*, concerns the gift to see in the material world the unity and harmony put there by the Divine Mind and carried out by the Logos present in those creatures by His activity. The final stage of contemplative gnosis is *theoria theologica* in which God is *heard*[30] in a direct encounter; no longer is He perceived through the created, physical world.

In this personal revelation by God to the individual, knowledge assimilates the person to God through love. This knowledge is not static, but is renovating, effecting a true ontological change in man's nature. Man reaches an ever increasing likeness to God which shows itself in "imitation of God as far as possible." The true Gnostic lives by God's self-revelation. He has displaced sin, self-centered *passionate* action with actions consciously willed by him because God so wills such. Clement describes the Gnostic:

He is the Gnostic, who is after the image and likeness of God, who imitates God as far as possible, deficient in none of the things which contribute to the likeness as far as compatible, practising self-restraint and endurance, living righteously, reigning over the passions, bestowing of what he has as far as possible and doing good both by word and deed.[31]

The Gnostic imitates God, especially in doing good to others with no thought of reward to self. "But only the doing of good out of love and for the sake of its own excellence is to be the Gnostic's choice."[32]

The Gnostic is characterized by Clement firstly as a completely integrated being in God through impassibility (*apatheia*). Christ the perfect Gnostic is the example for men.

The Gnostic is such, that he is subject only to the affections that exist for the maintenance of the body, such as hunger, thirst and the like . . . Christ was entirely impassible (*apathes*); inaccessible to any movement of feeling—either of pleasure or pain. While the Apostles, having most gnostically mastered, through the Lord's teaching, anger and fear and lust, were not liable even to such of the movements of feeling as seem good, courage, zeal, joy, desire through a steady condition of mind, not changing a whit; but ever continuing unvarying in a state of training after the resurrection of the Lord.[33]

The other trait of the Gnostic and surely the more perfect is that of love for God. He "possesses beauty by love"[34]; hence no longer delights in "small and grovelling things."[35] Love is fed by the faith and hope that make of the Gnostic, already possessing within himself the object of all his desires, God Himself, a divinized creature.

> For love is not desire on the part of him who loves; but it is a relation of affection, restoring the Gnostic to the unity of the faith—independent of time and place. But he who by love is already in the midst of that in which he is destined to be, and has anticipated hope by knowledge, does not desire anything, having, as far as possible, the very thing desired. Accordingly, as to be expected, he continues in the exercise of gnostic love, in the one unvarying state.[36]

We see that this state of *gnosis* is a mystical union that surpasses man's natural powers to attain. God is stamped on the Gnostic, permitting him to "live well." Thus God gives the Gnostic the power to pray in thought perpetually through the constant union of love with God. He understands the true meaning of sin and how to ask for forgiveness. He has the "power of well-doing and of comprehending the whole creation and administration by the Lord, that, becoming pure in heart through the knowledge, which is by the Son of God, he may be initiated into the beatific vision face to face . . . .[37]

Clement does not speculate as to the mystery of this divine assimilation that takes place in man. He is content to assert the fact and to describe it, again in intellectual terms of contemplation and prophecy:

> . . . a divine power of goodness clinging to the righteous soul in contemplation and prophecy and in the exercise of the function of governing, impresses on it something, as it were, of intellectual radiance, like the solar ray, as a visible sign of righteousness, uniting the soul with light,

through unbroken love, which is God-bearing and God-borne. Thence assimilation to God the Savior comes to the Gnostic as far as permitted to human nature, he being made perfect 'as the Father who is in heaven'.[38]

This is the vision of divinization that Clement holds out to the Christian, striving for perfection. Its fulfillment is attained only in the final beatific vision. The words of R. B. Tollington best summarize Clement's view on image and likeness:

Both in love and in understanding there is a certain identification of man's individual nature with the external fact or person, in so far as this is loved or understood. We are what we see. There is a certain kinship between the mind and what it apprehends. The final stage of vision, as Clement seems to conceive it, is the fulfillment of this principle in its completest term. We have already seen how the increasing likeness of the soul to God issues, at last, in a condition in which man *is* rather than resembles, the divine. It is the most intimate phase of his being's contact with supreme reality. It is more than knowledge, though it is less than ecstasy: "communion," perhaps, is the nearest equivalent in English, though the conception never loses a certain intellectualist tone. Man has intercourse with the divine and shares its holy nature. "The apprehensive vision of the pure in heart" is consummated in fellowship with God. "We close with all we love," and with all we know. It is the Pauline conception of "seeing face to face," the entire accord and harmony that unites the soul to its kindred environment. Language is a poor medium for portraying the final intimacy of the soul with God. There is more, Clement knows, than he can say; it is significant that he can only conduct the spiritual traveler up to the vestibule of the sanctuary. The great High Priest must do the rest.[39]

CHAPTER FIVE
ORIGEN

Origen, the first truly speculative theologian of the early Church who tried to organize the traditional tenets of the Christian Creed into an evolved theological system, was born in Alexandria in the year 185. At the early age of 18, he succeeded his master, Clement, as head of the catechetical school of Alexandria. In 215 he left this to found a school of superior learning that antedated the medieval universities. Here he used all profane sciences, Hellenic culture and philosophy to clarify and develop Christian doctrine. Some writers consider him one of the most fertile minds in human history; few dispute that he was one of the most prolific. He came at a period of history that beckoned to a trail blazer of original thought and synthesis. Origen filled the need in the early Church by excelling as the first great speculative theologian, biblical exegete, apologist, ascetical and mystical writer.

Origen also synthesized his theology and asceticism around the structure of the image and likeness of God in man with a thoroughness and consistency unknown in the writers before him.[1] He thus prepared the way for a more precise formulation by the Greek Fathers that followed him in the 4th and 5th centuries. Using the same structure of image and likeness, we can well synopsize Origen's entire theological systematization.

MAN CREATED "ACCORDING TO THE IMAGE" OF GOD

As his teacher, Clement of Alexandria, so Origen, in speaking of man, creates an anthropology centered around the Divine Logos as the revealer of a saving *gnosis*. Along with St. Paul, Origen affirms that Jesus Christ alone is the perfect image of God, His wisdom, the reflection of His perfection and glory, the invisible Image of God.[2] He insists on the same incorporeality of the Logos as of the Father because of the sameness of divine nature. Appealing to the invisibility of the Image expressed by St. Paul and the statement of St. John that no one has ever seen God,[3] Origen argues:

> To see is one thing, to know is another. To see and to have seen, this is proper to bodies; to know and to be known are of the intellectual order. All this that is proper to bodies must not be attributed to the Father, neither to the Son. What pertains to the nature of divinity we must affirm of the Father and the Son. This is why John in his Gospel does not say that no one has *seen* the Father but the Son, nor seen the Son but the Father; rather, he says that no one but the Father *knows* the Son and it is the Son who alone knows the Father . . .[4] Since one cannot properly use the words to see and be seen in dealing with an incorporeal and invisible nature, the Gospel does not say that the Father is seen through the Son nor the Son through the Father, but that they are known one through the other.[5]

As there is nothing corporeal in the Divine Logos, He is really God, for only God is immortal and incorruptible since only God is incorporeal. He proceeds from the Father, not by division (possible only with corporeal beings) but by a spiritual, eternal act of generation.[6] The Logos therefore exists from all eternity, outside of time.[7] He is "not a son through adoption, but a son by nature."[8] He flows eternally from the divine substance itself. Thus

Origen pioneers the crucial word for the later Council of Nicaea (325), *homoousios*, in comparing the outflow from Father to Son as of the same substance.

> For an outflow seems *homoousios*, that is,
> of one substance with that body of which
> it is the outflow or exhalation.[9]

Origen then compares this Logos, the Image of God the Father, to another image, man himself. The Divine Logos is the perfect and immediate Image of God, being of the same substance with the Father while man is an imperfect and mediate image of God. The Logos is the intermediate between God the Father and man. Thus man has been made "according to the image," that is, immediately modeled on the Logos, Jesus Christ, and only mediately, through the intercession of the Logos, created according to the Image that is God the Father.

The reasoning of Origen is seen in his theory of the double creation of man as he interprets the narration in Genesis.[10] In the first account of Genesis we learn that God Himself spoke: "Let us make mankind in our image and likeness." And "God created man in His image. In the image of God He created him, male and female He created them."[11] This Origen interprets allegorically to refer to the creation of man's soul, that which has been in God's image.

In the second account of Genesis. "The Lord God formed man out of the dust of the ground and breathed into his nostrils the breath of life and man became a living being."[12] This serves Origen as the basis for his cosmology. According to his speculation on man's creation, Origen teaches a doctrine of preexistence of human souls. These souls are pure spirits (*noes*). The fall mentioned in Genesis symbolizes the degradation of these human souls by disobedience to God's commands. Origen traces the meaning of soul (*psyche*) to the verb:

psychesthai—to grow cold.[13] These human souls grew cold in their love for God; hence they fell from God. God created the material world as a place of purification for these human souls. Therefore Origen interprets the second account of creation as the creation of a material body into which has been consigned the human soul. The differences in grace found among men are explained by the degrees of turning away from God to become immersed in matter, the principle of multiplicity and potency.

Origen finds in St. Paul's formula of the "interior" and "exterior" man[14] a confirmation of his interpretation of Genesis: The interior man is the human soul, made (*poiein*) by God "according to the image" of God. The exterior man is not made, but fashioned (*plattein*).[15] Thus the real man is the soul, for here we find man truly made "according to the image" of God. The image, contrary to St. Irenaeus' doctrine, is not found in the body of man. The image of God, in its fundamental meaning, can never say a reference to a corporeal body. The following text of Origen clearly sets forth this doctrine:

> It is not the fashioned body which contains the image. Corporeal man is not said to have been made but fashioned as it is in effect implied, as though (in Genesis) it is said: 'And God fashioned man from the slime of the earth. He who was made according to the image is our interior man, invisible, incorporeal, incorruptible and immortal.[16]

Origen in such speculation is following consistently his basic principle of God's utter transcendence from all potency. God, incorporeal, could have no relation whatsoever to limiting matter. He argues somewhat naively that, if the image of God is to be found both in man's soul and body, then

God Himself would be a composite, equally constituted of a principle of potency, body, and the
soul, the incorporeal principle. Origen is not re-
jecting the body as though it were the source of
all corruption and of all evil, but, in his single-
mindedness, he over-stresses the dignity of man as
"according to the image" of God to consist in the
incorporeality of the soul.

He offers other texts to show that more precisely the image is located in man's higher faculty
of the soul, his intellect (*nous*). His reasoning
again, following that of Clement of Alexandria and
the Platonic philosophy, is that it is the intellect
that allows man to understand God and therefore
through this knowledge (*gnosis*) man can be assimilated to the object that he knows. Origen maintains therefore the Platonic triple division in man:
nous is the *pneuma* or spirit, created by God in the
beginning. It had a pre-existence before man's
animal soul (*psyche*) and his body (soma) were
fashioned out of matter.[17] The image of God in man
is for Origen the *nous*, sometimes called by him the
logos, sometimes the faculty of the soul (*hegemoni-
kon*).[18] Man's imaging of God therefore resides in
his highest element, the spirit that allows him to
know God and in this same spirit to love Him.

SIN AND THE IMAGE

We have already pointed out that the immersion of the human spirit into an animal soul, the
seat of all passions, and into the material body was
considered by Origen the result of a free turning
away by the human spirit from God. Therefore
every human spirit, for Origen, except that of
Jesus, has become clothed with a body as a result
of a freely willed defection.[19] But this poses a difficulty in regard to Adam and his fall. In this

matter we see the fertile mind of Origen searching ever for new speculative formulations. A. Slomkowski outlines several of Origen's views on the role of Adam and the nature of Original Sin.[20] Speaking as a Platonist, Origen sees the body as a habitat for the soul. in which the soul can return through purifications to its former state of spiritual existence.[21] He speaks another language in preaching to the simple faithful as he presents the biblical account of Adam's formation and fall as history. Lastly, in writing for learned people, he allegorizes the Genesis account to the point that Adam stands merely symbolically as a philosophical view of humanity.

In his speculation where he treats Adam as an historical reality, Origen does grant to Adam a condition superior to ours. Adam possessed gifts of immortality and incorruptibility (in the traditional patristic language this was the usual way of speaking about a shared divine life).[22] Adam seemed to possess a relative perfection and a *righteousness*.[23] He possessed as distinct both the *image* (*eikon*) and the *likeness* (*homoiosis*). By reason of his intellectual soul (*nous*), Adam was *kat 'eikona*, made "according to the image" of God.[24] He possessed the *likeness* (*homoiosis*), not as a static perfection, but as a dynamic orientation to a greater likeness of God by assimilation to His nature through "imitation of God."[25] To continuously grow in this likeness Adam had to turn towards the image and imitate God by living according to the spirit and not according to matter, the principle of potency and delimitation in being.[26]

Adam by sin lost his privileges and all of his posterity similarly was confined to matter as to the principle that delimited man in his thrust to *become* more of being. Yet man still possesses the divine spark in his intellect, the seat of the image of God in man. By living according to the true, invisible

Image of God, the Divine Logos, man's logos, his intellect, may recuperate the likeness to God, lost by sin.

IMAGE AND LIKENESS

Some of Origen's texts present these two terms as synonymous.[27] Usually however, *image* means a basic relationship to God received at creation and somehow obscured through the fall and man's personal sins.[28] Likeness or *homoiosis* is on another plane, yet unfolds in and through the image-spirit.

Origen's distinction between image and likeness is clearly seen in a passage from his *De Principis*:

> . . . 'And God said, Let us make man in our own image and after our likeness;' and then he adds the words: 'So God created man in His own image, in the image of God created He him; male and female created He them and He blessed them.' Now the expression, 'in the image of God created He him,' without any mention of the word 'likeness,' conveys no other meaning than this, that man received the dignity of God's image at his first creation; but that the perfection of his likeness has been reserved for the consummation,— namely, that he might acquire it for himself by the exercise of his own diligence in the imitation of God, the possibility of attaining to perfection being granted him at the beginning through the dignity of the divine image, and the perfect realization of the divine likeness being reached in the end by the fulfillment of the (necessary) works.[29]

Likeness says a direct relationship to the Logos who alone is capable of returning the human image to a correspondence to His own perfect relationship of knowledge and love of the Father. Only through the Divine Word is the release from matter, as from the principle of potency, possible, thus opening man to the fullness of his being as destined by God's original creation. The Logos therefore for Origen is necessary that man be most perfectly man, for he is man substantially insofar as he possesses a *nous*-intellect, capable of knowing the Source of all being and a will capable of loving that Source.

> At all times through His word . . . God
> has placed on the good path those who
> lend an ear to His words.[30]

ROLE OF THE LOGOS

As man's immersion in matter or potency (distance from God, the Source of all act of being) is determined by his free turning away from God, redemption is conceived by Origen as a return through the intermediation of the Logos to the original state of spirit from which man fell. In his basic principle "the end is always like the beginning,"[31] we see the influence of Stoicism's recirculation of all creatures back to their original state. Yet in the application of his principle he shows his true Christianity as opposed to the rigid "return" of creatures proposed by the Stoics by affirming that the return to the original state is not a mere mechanical return to the equality in which all human spirits were created, but God's grace and man's willed cooperation determine different degrees of possessing the goal. Cadiou thus calls his theory "a Platonic myth."[32] To describe this process of return to the original state of man-spirit, Origen uses the word, *apokatastasis*, meaning a restoration to a former condition. The role of Christ in bringing about the redemption of mankind is conceived primarily as that of a teacher. Evil, conceived as the lack of due perfection in a being, hence intimately associated with matter, as the principle of potency, would eventually disappear. All men would eventually reach their destined goal since Origen views sanctity as a matter of sufficient knowledge. God uses the whole material world with all the evil inherent in it to educate us away from our fallen selves back to the dignity that once was ours, as sons of God. Origen views our redemption under a double aspect: the traditional doctrine of faith that Christ by His human life of obedience to His Heavenly Father's will, especially as climaxed in His death on the Cross, has conquered over the evil powers that hold the cosmos in their hands. This was Paul's way of conceiving Christ's victory over a personalized enemy, Satan. The other side of our redemption consisted in Christ, the Divine Logos, instructing us in our radical insufficiency before the Heavenly Father. Guided by God's infinite love for mankind and man's free will, Origen taught that the only complete fulfillment of God's purpose in creating human spirits according to His Image, Christ the Logos, would be attained only when all created spirits would eventually acknowledge His supremacy and love Him for Himself. The time will come, as Paul insisted, when God will be all in all (I Cor. 15, 28), when the whole of creation will reach its fulfillment, or, viewed by Origen from God's Mind, restored to its original integrity.[33]

The Fifth General Council, Constantinople II (553), condemned the doctrine of *apokatastasis* in these words: "If anyone teaches the mythical doctrine of the pre-existence of the soul and the apokatastasis that follows from it, let him be anathema" (Canon I). What this canon condemns is that human souls pre-existed before the existence of the human bodies and that all human beings must eventually be saved. Clearly, the cosmic doctrine exposed by St. Paul and St. Irenaeus that Christ will recapitulate in the Parousia all things (Eph. 1, 10) was not condemned. How this will be done will remain a mystery, but Origen had the temerity to speculate by stressing the mercy of God finally winning all men back to Him and the eventual disappearance of evil.

We find at the basis of the writings of Origen Clement's whole theory of gnosis. It aims at a deeper understanding of the faith, an effort in all things to look beyond the sensible appearances of material phenomena in an attempt to penetrate to the inner *reality*. Little stress (as compared to Irenaeus) is placed on the Incarnation mainly because the visible is no more than a sacrament of the invisible Christ who had been working in the entire universe from the beginning of time. The actual appearance on this earth of the humanity of Christ is simply a means of contacting the Logos. Visible phenomena of Christianity are shadows and prophecies of things yet to come. The historical Christ is a sacrament revealing the inner Logos-Christ who presides over the inner life, present but unseen in the Church and in our souls. Both in Scripture, in the whole material universe and in the individual life of us there are the somatic, psychic and pneumatic experiences in knowledge.[34] We find the Logos revealing Himself to us on different levels according to our capabilities which are made actual by our purification and sense knowledge. The *somatic* is the literal sense of phenomena which manifest to us God in His activity in our world by revealing Himself through the written literal word, through nature or through the individual experience of the soul. *Psychic* is the moral sense that we derive beyond the literal interpretation. The highest, the *pneumatic*, is the spiritual sense, the mind of God hidden beyond the phenomena. Through an infused gnosis, one's speculative and practical intellect is brought to resemble the mind of Christ. Christ is virtue and by living virtuously, one lives in Christ. The gnosis brings about a resemblance and imitation of Christ. To be in Christ means to be immersed in Christ. Though difficult to describe, this union with Christ is nonetheless real. It is not simply to model ourselves on the example of Christ, but it is to allow the Master, the Teacher (*didaskalos*), present to teach, to reveal Himself, the Logos, the summation of all reality, to us.

Origen develops a whole spirituality of the Logos around Christ as the intermediary between absolute unity of the Trinity and multiplicity of creatures, going at times to the extent of apparently subordinating Christ to God the Father. Redemption lies in Christ's victory over the powers of evil that hold mankind in captivity. The world is regarded by Origen as the scene of the great educative process carried on by the Logos, the Master and Healer that gradually illuminates free creatures to return to the good. Everything in life is a means of education. The universe is a vast *didaskaleion* or university in which every single thing contributes to the education of free human beings.[35]

The first step in associating with Jesus Christ in the process of deification is faith (pre-supposing Baptism which has already remitted sin) which is affirmed and grows by a Christian life.[36] Yet here begins the process of sanctification that admits of a great diversity in perfection. As Clement, Origen distinguishes two classes of Christians: the simple mass of believers, "friends of the letter" who are content with the literal meaning of Holy Scripture and the surface of the Christian mysteries. These know Jesus Christ crucified and esteem the Logos become flesh, but like the Pauline Corinthians, they are fed milk like infants. "Christ pastures them because of their sweet and docile natures but not because they are intelligent."[37] But the "more intelligent," the elite or perfect, participate in the Logos by being granted the *gnosis*. Guided by the Logos, these *teleioumenoi* or perfect Christians leave the sensible things of creation to acquire firstly a knowledge of the intelligent cosmos, then of the Logos Himself;[38] finally they arrive at a contemplation of the essence of the power of God Himself.[39] This *gnosis* is a gift of God, surpassing all human nature, that "God gives to those who have rendered themselves apt to receive it."[40] In lyrical terms Origen exalts this unitive *gnosis* wherein the Logos inebriates us "in drawing us from human things, He fills us with enthusiasm and enervates us with a drunkenness which is not irrational but divine."[41] With such metaphors Origen shows that his mystical union leads to ecstasy, at least in the final stage of the Beatific Vision. In the superior part of man's being he is assumed into the order of angels. "The souls of these men are assumed in consequence of their moral progress into the order of angels."[42]

Thus we see that the chief work of the Logos present in man's soul is to raise him to the true knowledge about Himself and the Trinity by which knowledge man shares in the life of the Father. Yet the degree to which the Logos enlightens man is related to and proportioned to the merits and love of the individual. The work of man's elevation is therefore not exclusively intellectual, but moral and voluntary as well. As preliminary to Christ's infusion of God's knowledge and life man must purge his soul, prescind from his material part and thus regain the true image of God and arrive at a likeness to God.[43] It is the Holy Spirit that is the principal agent in effecting this transformation in us of the image to the likeness, of the seed to the full-grown son, from present participation to future possession in fullness.

THE ENERGIZED PRESENCE OF
THE HOLY SPIRIT AS GRACE

The pedagogical work of the Logos in our souls is carried on through the Holy Spirit. Man walks "in the newness of life" (Rom. 9, 17) "so that he might receive the new wine, the newness of the grace of the Holy Spirit."[44] We are capable of receiving Christ in the degree that we have been sanctified by the Holy Spirit.

> . . . When therefore rational beings obtain first their existence from God the Father, then their rational nature from the Word, and thirdly their holiness from the Holy Spirit, they are made capable of receiving Christ in His capacity of Righteousness, because they have now been sanctified through the Holy Spirit; and those who have merited the attainment of this degree of progress through the sanctification of the Holy Spirit obtain just as surely the gift of wisdom through the power of the working of the Spirit of God . . . . That . . . those who were made by God may be present unceasingly and inseparably with Him who is, it is the work of wisdom to instruct and educate them and lead them to perfection, by the strengthening and the unceasing sanctification of the Holy Spirit, through which sanctification alone they can attain to God.[45]

Thus the Holy Spirit comes to those who are already open to God's operations. Those receiving the Holy Spirit receive Him according to the capacity that God gives them. Yet this capacity is proportionate to their faith in Christ and their thirsting after and longing for God. Those lives are praiseworthy for their good deeds, virtues and love and to them the Holy Spirit comes and indwells. ". . . the Holy Spirit, from whom those who thirst after and long for God obtain 'spiritual graces' (Rom. I, II) and heavenly gifts."[46] The operations of the Holy Spirit are seen especially in prayer. Man of his own cannot understand the sublimity of prayer nor pray as he ought. Before we can pray as Jesus prayed we must be taught by Him and hear the prayer of the Holy Spirit within us. Because of His love for us He makes up the failings of our prayers. He intercedes for us with the Father depending upon the intensity of our virtuous life.[47]

Therefore we can say that for Origen the Holy Spirit is the *dinamis*, the power of God working within us to deify us into the likeness of God. He does this intellectually by leading our minds to the Son and the Father. He infuses us with the interior knowledge of the nature and faith of the Trinity. The Father is revealed by the Son but all knowledge and unitive love of the Father are gained in the Holy Spirit. In the moral area of virtues the Holy Spirit spurs us on to bring forth fruits of good works or of virtuous deeds. The most perfect good work is that of prayer and here we see a whole theology of the graceful working of the Holy Spirit within us teaching us how to pray properly and making us capable of living the union attained through prayer perpetually. The Christian progresses to divinization through the stages of conversion, rebirth in Christ, growth in this Divine Life (grace), culminating finally in perfection of the beatific vision.

FINAL TRANSFIGURATION INTO CHRIST

Although man in this life can through the sanctifying operations of the Holy Spirit participate in the likeness of God by possessing the life of the

Logos within him, nevertheless, it is only in the resurrectional life that man attains to the fullness of God's likeness.

Origen's thought on the final resurrection of man's body has been disputed down through the centuries. Jerome, Epiphanius and Theophilos all take Origen to task either for having denied the resurrection of the human body or for the confused manner in which he understood it.[48] Several modern authors, however, maintain strongly that Origen held the resurrection of the human body.[49]

In his preface to *De Principiis* in which he is careful to outline his beliefs of faith as he accepts them from the traditional Church, Origen teaches a resurrection of the body:

> After these points also the apostolic teaching is . . . that there is to be a time of resurrection from the dead, when this body which now 'is sown in corruption, shall rise in incorruption' and that which 'is sown in dishonor will rise in glory.' (I Cor. 15, 42-43)[50]

Crouzel does well in pointing out that Origen uses the word body and even flesh quite ambiguously, applying it sometimes to bodies in general and again only to the "terrestrial" bodies.[51] Taking his concept of matter from the current Neo-Platonism of his day, quite similar to that of Plotinus, Origen conceives matter as that which is pure potency, possessing no quality in itself but receiving and supporting qualities. Thus, although it is constantly undergoing change and renewal in a given being, there is a substratum that maintains a constant identity. This principle of permanence is not found in the matter of pure potency but in the "corporeal form."[52] Thus all created beings are *corporeal*, including angels, in this sense that they possess a corporeal form that is a principle of individuating identity. The resurrection, therefore, holds no great

82

difficulty for Origen for the "terrestrial" form, subject to concupiscence, will truly pass away only to be transfigured in the resurrection into a "celestial" form, yet the "corporeal" form will be the same and will insure identity with the individual being that has passed from his terrestrial to celestial existence.

In the final resurrection of men the full role of the Divine Logos will be clearly seen. In Baptism we have conformed ourselves partially to His resurrection by dying to concupiscences (the "terrestrial," diabolical images in man) and by rising to put on His glorified divine life. Only in the resurrection of the saved is there a full conformity to the death and resurrection of Christ. Origen argues that as Christ's body was resurrected and glorified and we are His brothers, of the same human nature as He possessed, so too our bodies will also be resurrected.[53] This is clearly illustrated in the following text on Origen's commentary on St. Matthew:

> All who are begotten from on high through water and the Spirit will be free from sin. Admittedly, their freedom will be, so to speak, like 'a confused reflection in a mirror' (I Cor. 13, 12); but when the Son of Man comes in glory and takes His seat on His throne, there will be a further rebirth; all who then are reborn in Christ will be quite free from sin—their freedom this time will be 'face to face.' And the reason why they have obtained this rebirth will be that they were previously reborn in the bath . . . When we are reborn of water, we are buried with Christ. When we are reborn . . . of fire and the Spirit, we shall become like Christ's body . . . on its throne in glory and we shall sit on the twelve thrones ourselves—at least, we shall

83

> if we have forsaken everything, through
> Baptism especially, and followed Him.[54]

We see the theology of Baptism given an eschatological dimension. It is through the first Baptism that man is again restored to the Divine likeness. It is in the eschatological purification of each saved soul that the second Baptism of purgatorial fire removes all blemish and dross and brings the image of God in man to its fullness.[55] All terrestrial concupiscences have been removed and man is completely celestial, conforming himself in his total being to the resurrected Christ.

In this perfect conformity Christ communicates His own divine life to the resurrected man. Man has now received the fullness according to his capacity of the likeness of God. In contemplating God face to face, man receives the form of God. Now man is perfectly assimilated into the likeness of God by the fullness of his *gnosis*. Those purified will be *educated* by God in the last mysteries.

> For He will show to them, as to children, the causes of things and the power of His creation . . . And so, when they have finished all those matters which are connected with the stars, and with the heavenly revolutions, they will come to those which are not seen, or to those whose names only we have heard, and to things which are invisible, which the Apostle Paul has informed us are numerous . . . And thus the rational nature, growing by each individual step, not as it grew in this life in flesh and body and soul, but enlarged in understanding and in power of perception, is raised as a mind already perfect to perfect knowledge, no longer at all impeded by those carnal senses, but in-increased in intellectual growth; and ever gazing purely, and, so to speak, face to

face, on the causes of things, it attains perfection, firstly, that by which it ascends to
(the truth) and secondly that by which
it abides in it, having problems and the
understanding of things and the causes of
events as the food on which it may feast
. . . . The mind, when it has attained perfection, eats and avails itself of suitable
and appropriate food in such a degree, that
nothing ought to be either deficient or
superfluous. And in all things this food is
to be understood as the contemplation and
understanding of God which is a measure
appropriate and suitable to this nature
which was made and created.[56]

It is traditionally believed that Origen's theory
of *apokatastasis* demanded the ultimate salvation of
all men. Yet other texts of Origen, especially where
he insists on giving his beliefs in conformity to the
traditional teaching of the Church, prove that only
the justified will reach the fullness of the Beatific
Vision. The damned will not be given another chance
but will be sentenced to eternal punishment. This
seems clear from his preface to the *De Principiis*:

. . . the apostolic teaching is that the soul
. . . shall, after its departure from the
world, be rewarded according to its deserts,
being destined to obtain either an inheritance of eternal life and blessedness, if its
action shall have procured this for it, or
to be delivered up to eternal fire and pun-
ishments, if the guilt of its crimes shall
have brought it down to this.[57]

H. Crouzel offers a text that he claims as most
indisputably that of Origen which clearly denies
the ultimate salvation of the damned:

The saints who are in this habitation groan
heavily under the weight of the body of
humiliation and do all (necessary) in

> order to be judged worthy to be received
> into the mystery of the resurrection when
> God will transfigure the body of humilia-
> tion—not of all men, but the genuine dis-
> ciples of Christ in order to render them
> conformable to His body of glory.[58]

Thus the total man will be "conformable" to
the total, resurrected, glorious Jesus Christ. This
likeness will consist in possessing completely and
not partially as in this present life the divinity.
Only then does man become in fullness the son
of God, participating in the unity of immutability
of God Himself. Having put off the terrestrial "body
of humiliation," man will be clothed with a glorious
body. He will contemplate all beings through the
living Logos who will nourish man to understand
Truth itself. The *logoi* in all creatures will be
comprehended by glorified man. Man will see God
as He is and as the Son sees Him. No longer will
the Logos be the intermediary, our *didaskalos*.
Rather, He will assimilate us to Himself in a mysterious union where we, retaining our self-identity,
will be "of Him" in some interior way. In that
final union man made "according to the Image,"
that is, Jesus Christ, will reach the fullness of resemblance or likeness to God.

> Then all of those who will have reached
> God through the Word who is near Him,
> will engage in a unique activity—to comp-
> rehend God so that they, so formed in
> the knowledge of the Father, all together
> will become exactly one Son as now only
> the Son knows the Father.[59]

God will be all in all as the Logos brings His
work of revealing the Mind of the Heavenly Father
to a fullness. The individual man will retain his
autonomy—but the autonomy of man with the
ability to imitate the Logos in saying "Yes, Father,"
now reaches its perfection. Man freely wills for all

86

eternity to love God as Father in union with the love of the Divine Son to whose image man has been created. The created image has reached the goal of its growth in attaining a divinization that transfigures his life into God's life. The Logos has assimilated man to Himself. Origen's system of theological speculation on the image and likeness of God in man is climaxed in the words of St. Peter:

> See how all the gifts that make for life and holiness in us belong to His divine power; come to us through fuller knowledge of Him whose own glory and sovereignty have drawn us to Himself: Through Him God has bestowed on us high and treasured promises; you are to share the divine nature, with the world's corruption, the world's passions, left behind.[60]

CHAPTER SIX
SAINT ATHANASIUS

In a period of confused thinking on the basic dogmas of the Trinity and Christology, St. Anthanasius stood out as a shining beacon of orthodoxy. To him more than to any other Father of the early Church the title of Father of orthodoxy was universally accorded. In the innumerable attacks by the Arians against him personally that resulted in five exiles away from his see of Alexandria, through his innumerable writings, by his oratory in church councils, especially in the first Council of Nicaea, St. Anthanasius proved himself to be a true expositor of the Church's traditional teachings. Born about the year 295 and died in the year 373, Athanasius spent his long life in a continued controversy against the Arian heresy that had denied divinity to Jesus Christ. He did not possess the classical education or the love of Greek philosophy that Origen, Basil the Great, Gregory Nazianzen and Gregory of Nyssa possessed. He was primarily a pastor of sheep who needed to be defended from erroneous doctrines. Philosophy was helpful only to articulate more accurately the Church's teachings. His theology, especially the doctrine of the image of God in man, is more a result of circumstances that forced him to defend the faith against the erroneous doctrines of the Arian heretics, rather than a calmly composed system of theological speculation.[1] His whole pastoral life and theological writings are dominated by his controversy with Arianism; thus we can see that his image doctrine also will be developed according to his orientation.

THE DIVINE LOGOS—IMAGE OF THE FATHER[2]

St. Anthanasius inherited the problem that

haunted his whole life from Origen. The basic tenets of Origen, quite unsuspected by himself, prepared the way for the Arian heresy. Dr. T. E. Pollard maintains that Origen encountered difficulties with his Logos doctrine in maintaining a subordination- ism to the Father contrary to the traditional teach- ing of the Church on the equality of the Son of God in nature to the Father. Origen saw his dif- ficulties as running contrary to tradition, yet failed in his system to replace effectively the Logos con- cept with an adequate teaching on the Sonship.[3] The Arians tried to solve Origen's problem by dis- tinguishing between the Logos and the Son. The Son is not of the same nature as the Logos; He possesses the title Logos by grace or participation but is not of one and the same nature as the divine Logos. Athanasius gives us the Arians' distinction:

And (they say) 'Christ is not very God, but He, as others, was made God by par- ticipation.[4]

Against this heretical position, Athanasius at- tacked the Arians and proved the full divinity of Jesus Christ by showing that He is the same as the Divine Logos, the perfect Image of the Father (Col. 1, 15), possessing the same nature as the Father, *homoousion;* hence having absolute equality in *being* with the Father.

Athanasius begins his exposition of the orthodox teaching on the *homoousia,* of the same essence, of the Father and the Son, by proving that the Son is the Image of the Father. His basic thinking is: if the Son is the perfect Image of the Father, He must be the same nature as the Father.

We may perceive this at once from the illustration of the emperor's image. For in the image is the shape and form of the emperor and in the emperor is that shape which is in the image. For the likeness of the emperor in the image is exact; so that a person, who looks at the image, sees in it the emperor; and he again, who sees the emperor, recognizes that it is he who is in the image. And from the likeness not differing, to one who after the image wished to view the emperor, the image might say, 'I and the emperor are one; for I am in him and he is in me; and what thou seest in me, that thou beholdest in him.' Accordingly he who worships the image, in it worships the emperor also, for the image is his form and appearance. Since then the Son too is the Father's Image, it must necessarily be understood that the Godhead and propriety of the Father is the Being of the Son.[5]

If the Son is the Image of the Father and hence mirrors forth perfectly the same substance of the Father, it follows that whatever can be predicated of the Father can be also said of the Son. Athanasius follows this reasoning with the conclusion that the Son, being the Image of the Invisible God, is also, *qua Image*, invisible. The Logos-Image is eternal and transcendent, referring to the interior Trinitarian life. The Logos as Image of the Father is outside of a time-space relationship to His temporal incarnational mission.

Athanasius makes as his own doctrine Origen's exegesis of Col. 1, 15 in establishing that the Image is indeed invisible and from all eternity; hence co-equal with the Father:

If there be an Image of the invisible God, it is an invisible Image; nay, I will be bold to add, that, as being the likeness of the Father, never was it not. For when was that God, who, according to John, is called Light (for 'God is Light'), without a radiance of His proper glory, that a man should presume to assert the Son's origin of existence, as if before He was not? But when was not that Image of the Father's Ineffable and Nameless and Unutterable Subsistence, that Expression and Word, and He that knows the Father? For let him understand well who dares to say, 'Once the Son was not', that he is saying, 'Once Wisdom was not,' and 'Word was not.' and 'Life was not.'[6]

In this strict usage of Image as applied to the uncreated, eternal Logos, Athanasius veers away from Paul's evidently implied role of the Logos as manifesting to creatures the invisible Father. Thus we see a basic difference between his image doctrine and that of St. Irenaeus. As has been already pointed out in Chapter III, Irenaeus puts great stress on the Incarnate Logos as the invisible God made visible. Hence his Logos is seen more in relationship to finite man needing a visible model of perfection as the way back to *recapitulation* rather than in the pure essence of the Logos Himself. For Athanasius, the Logos or Divine Word is the Image of the Father, saying no immediate relationship to the created order but used by Athanasius purely to conclude that therefore He is like the Father in the same essence.

The Image of Father which is the Logos is St. Athanasius' theological structure around which he shows that the Image is the total, perfect communication of the eternal Father who is immutable and indivisible. The Father and the Son are of the same nature. The Logos is the *ontos on*, the really real, *unparticipated* being, who enjoys the fulness of being from His very nature of Son. In being Son, He does not *participate* in the nature of the Father but possesses by nature the same being as His Father. Having well established the sameness of substance between the Father and the Son, Athanasius considers the relationship between the transcendent Logos and human beings.

IMAGE AND "ACCORDING TO THE IMAGE"

It has already been shown that Irenaeus, Clement and Origen all distinguished between image and likeness of God in man. For these early Fathers, man by nature is made to the image of God. Athanasius shows originality in his consistent affirmation that man is not an image of God, but that he is made "according to the Image" (*kat'eikona*). Having established that only the Divine Logos is the Image of God by nature, Athanasius insists that man could only be created according to the Logos, the Image. The *Image* of God does not *participate* in God's nature. He possesses it by His nature.

> And being the good Offspring of Him that is good, and being the true Son, He is the Father's Power and Wisdom and Word, not being so by participation, nor as if these qualities were imparted to Him from without, as they are to those who partake of Him and are made wise by Him and receive power and reason in Him; but He is the very Wisdom, very Word and very own Power of the Father . . . . And to sum all up, He is the wholly perfect Fruit of the Father and is alone the Son and unchanging Image of the Father.[7]

As Regis Bernard points out,[8] these ideas were expressed already by Irenaeus, Clement and Origen, but it was Athanasius who first fixed the two terms. Image (*eikon*) as applicable only to the Divine

Logos and "according to the Image" (kat'eikona) as
referring to human beings. Men for Athanasius "are
not themselves images" of God,[9] but are "made
after an image," that is, the Divine Son. The earlier
writers applied image and "according to the image"
to man as synonyms. Image for Athanasius now
refers only to the Divine Son and implies the same
substance with the Father. "According to the Image"
refers only to human beings and implies the participation of God's life in and through the instrumentality of Jesus Christ, the perfect Image.

Kat'eikona places the stress on man's participation in the nature of God, made possible only because of man's created relationship to the Logos
who, not by participation, but by His very nature,
is God. This participation Athanasius summarizes
thus:

> . . . being God, God gives them (men) a
> share in His own Image, our Lord Jesus
> Christ, and makes them after His own
> Image and after His likeness; so that by
> such grace perceiving the Image, that is,
> the Word of the Father, they may be able
> through Him to get an idea of the Father,
> and knowing their Maker, live the happy
> and truly blessed life.[10]

EFFECTS OF SIN

Athanasius places emphasis in dealing with sin
on its intrinsic essence, rather than the disruptive
act in history. In his attempt to show the meta-
physical nature of sin, he describes it as a turning
away from the contemplation of the Logos, as a
forgetting and a neglecting of the true nature of
man to be *kat'eikona*, according to the Image-
Christ.

> . . . so turning away and forgetting that

she (the human soul) was in the image of the good God, she no longer, by the power which is in her, sees God the Word after whose likeness she is made; but having departed from herself, images and feigns what is not. For hiding, by the complications of bodily lusts, the mirror which, as it were, is in her, by which alone she had the power of seeing the Image of the Father, she no longer sees what a soul ought to behold, but is carried about by everything and only sees the things which come under the senses.[11]

The first man, Adam, had been transfigured by the inhabitation of the Logos into His own image. The *kat'eikona* given to our first parents according to Athanasius was more than the indestructible image that his predecessors had bequeathed to man even after sin. This "according to the Image" was a gratuitous gift that included all that we term by the supernatural. We see that this "according to the Image" is an after-gift of God to the first parents, given beyond their basic human nature:

He gave them a further gift, and He did not barely create man, as He did all the irrational creatures on the earth, but made them after His own image, giving them a portion even of the power of His own Word; so that as it were having a kind of reflection of the Word, and being made rational, they might be able to abide ever in blessedness . . . .[12]

But God knew the weakness of man so He gave as a protection to the grace (referring to the *kat'-eikona*) the law imposed on man in Paradise and circumscribed him in a place wherein he would work out his salvation. If men kept the *grace* and grew according to the Image-Logos, they would continue to enjoy a life without "sorrow, pain or care" and would eventually receive the promise of incorruption with God in eternal Heaven.

> For man is by nature mortal, inasmuch as he is made out of what is not; but by reason of His likeness to Him that is (and if he still preserved this likeness by keeping Him in his knowledge) he would stay his natural corruption and remain incorrupt.[13]

But the awful fact of sin is one of the greatest realities for Athanasius. Man freely sinned by turning away from God; he allowed, through his yielding to concupiscences, the Image within him to become obscured. In discussing the fate of the *kat'-eikona* after the destructive effects of sin, Athanasius takes two diverse approaches.

In the first approach, especially in writing about pagans, he wishes to show that the "according to the Image" is not lost. Sin covers it over. It becomes more difficult for man to contemplate the perfect model of a virtuous life, the Logos. Fallen man can hardly see God in creation. The human soul forgets that "she was in the image of the good God, she no longer . . . sees God the Word after whose likeness she is made."[14]

The indestructibility of the image of God in man is brought out clearly in a passage that Athanasius cites to highlight the necessity of the Incarnation of the Word. Here he shows that the lineaments of the Logos-Image remain in spite of sin. Christ came to restore or renew the outline that had been dimmed through sin:

> For, as when the likeness painted on a panel has been effaced by stains from without, he whose likeness it is must needs come once more to enable the portrait to be renewed on the same wood; for, for the sake of his picture, even the mere wood on which it is painted is not thrown away,

but the outline is renewed upon it; in the same way also the most Holy Son of the Father, being the image of the Father, came to our region to renew man once made in His likeness and find him as one lost.[15]

The other approach which shows a lack of precision in Athanasius' anthropology puts the stress on the absolute necessity in the actual history of salvation of the Incarnate Word. The *Verbum caro factum est* was necessary because through sin, corruption and death reigned. Sin has stripped man of the grace, the *kat'eikona* and man fell into, not only natural corruption, but also into the destruction of the divine life of the Logos in his soul. Here we see the accent placed on the complete destruction of the "according to the Image" of God in man in order to highlight the radical opposition between sin and grace, death and life, corruption and incorruption, the devil and Christ the Conqueror.

But men, having despised and rejected the contemplation of God, and devised and contrived evil for themselves . . . received the condemnation of death with which they had been threatened; and from thenceforth no longer remained as they were made, but were being corrupted according to their devices; and death had the mastery over them as king. For transgression of the commandment was turning them back to their natural state, so that just as they have had their being out of nothing, so also, as might be expected, they might look for corruption into nothing in the course of time.[16]

Man, thus envisioned by Athanasius in the "natural state" without God's freely given gift of the "according to the Image," was being corrupted and was wasting away.

For this cause, then, death having gained upon men, and corruption abiding upon them, the race of man was perishing; the rational man made in God's image was disappearing and the handiwork of God was in process of dissolution.[17]

Athanasius thus prepares the stage for the entrance of the Incarnate Word. He reasons that it would not be according to God's wisdom to allow that creatures, once made rational and having partaken of the Word, should go to ruin and turn to non-existence. He argues that God could not allow His creation to go to neglect and ruin:

So, as the rational creatures were wasting and such works in course of ruin what was God in His goodness to do? Suffer corruption to prevail against them and death to hold them fast? . . . Neglect reveals weakness and not goodness on God's part —if, that is, He allows His own work to be ruined when once He had made it—more so than if He had never made man at all . . . but once He had made them and created them out of nothing, it were most monstrous for the work to be ruined and that before the eyes of the Maker.[18]

Over and over again in his chief dogmatic work, *De Incarnatione*, Athanasius reasons that God could not leave His human creatures, originally made according to the Divine Logos, under the corruptible hand of Satan. "What was God to do?" asks Athanasius. He could only recreate the lost relationship to the Divine Image and destroy corruptible death:

What was to be done save the renewing of that which was in God's image, so that by it men might once more be able to know Him? But how could this come to pass save by the presence of the very Image of God, our Lord Jesus Christ? For by men's means it was impossible, since they are but made after an image. Whence the Word of God came in His own person, that, as He was the Image of the Father, He might be able to create afresh the man after the image. But, again, it could not else have taken place had not death and corruption been done away. Whence he took in natural fitness a mortal body, that while death might in it be once for all done away, men made after His Image might once more be renewed. None other then was sufficient for this need, save the Image of the Father.[19]

Athanasius clearly shows that man of himself is incapable of recreating the image lost within him. It is only the Divine Word that could bring to re-birth that which in man was "according to His Image." Even in the first approach where Athanasius emphasizes the permanence of the image in man even after sin, he avoids a Pelagian position by the careful usage of the word *anakainizo*, to renew, make new.[20] This renewal of the image is not a mere removal of the obstructing layers that can be effected by man alone through his personal repentance. There must be a rebirth and a recreation back again into the *kat'eikona*. Yet this quality or state of relationship with the Divine Logos could be restored only by the real participated presence of the Logos, inhabiting man's soul. By taking a human body, Christ was able to reveal God Himself to man and thus, enlightening him, could lead him back to true wisdom.[21] Through His body the Divine Logos would die and conquer death. Thus His resurrectional life could be united to the human life of man still on this earth. Man could, through this intimate union in Divine life, be "recreated" according to the Image of the Divine Logos.[22]

DIVINIZATION OF MAN

One of the most consistent ways in which Athanasius presents his image doctrine is in his teaching on the divinization or deification of man. It was St. Irenaeus who first succinctly summarized the reason for the Incarnation. God became man in order that man might become God.[23] Athanasius uses the concept of man's divinization through Christ as a true synthetic principle in which also the divinizing activity of the Holy Spirit is clearly highlighted. Because of his consistent usage of this principle without much explanation, we can deduce that the concept of man's divinization through Christ's incarnational life was universally accepted, even by the heretics, such as the Arians. For starting from this base, as we shall see, Athanasius seeks to prove both the divinity of Jesus Christ against the Arian heretics and the divinity of the Holy Spirit against the *Pneumatomachoi*.

Athanasius never loses this principle that the end of the Incarnation is to deify fallen man. "For He was made man that we might be made God."[24] Again in his letter to Adelphius, Athanasius repeats his principle: "For He has become man that He might deify us in Himself."[25] In another letter, to Maximus, the same formula is used but applied to the Holy Eucharist:

We are deified, not by partaking of the body of some man, but by receiving the Body of the Word Himself.[26]

Arguing more precisely against the Arians in the Councils of Ariminum and Seleucia, Athanasius uses this principle to prove the divinity of Christ:

It follows that He, being the deifying and enlightening power of the Father, in which all things are deified and quickened, is not alien in essence from the Father, but co-essential. For by partaking of Him, we partake of the Father; because the Word is the Father's own. Whence, if He was Himself too from participation, and not from the Father, His essential Godhead and Image, He would not deify, being deified Himself.[27]

One remaining text similar to the above citations is found in the second discourse against the Arians in which Athanasius argues to the divinity of Christ through His divinization of man:

For therefore did He assume the body originate and human, that having renewed it as its Framer, He might deify it in Himself, and thus might introduce us all into the Kingdom of Heaven after His likeness. For man had not been deified if joined to a creature, unless the Son were very God; nor had man been brought into the Father's presence, unless He had been His natural and true Word who had put on the body.[28]

In all of these texts Athanasius uses a verb form from the word, *theopoiein* or its cognate noun, *theopoiesis*, meaning, to deify, or the work of divinizing. In treating of Clement of Alexandria, it was pointed out that he first introduced this unbiblical term. Athanasius canonized it as a synonym for the incarnational activity of the Word-made-flesh.

Not content to reestablish man to his original state, as Origen stressed, Jesus Christ, according to Athanasius, brings to man the grace of divinization which is an advance upon the original state of man. In thus presenting the unique role of the Incarnate Word in the dynamic terms of Irenaeus and the

Antiochene school as opposed to that of Origen's Alexandrian school, Athanasius has highlighted again the absolute necessity of the Incarnation. Jesus Christ is the necessary means to complete man's potentialities that in the first Adam were indicated by Athanasius' specific term of *kat'eikona*. The fulfilment of the "according to the Image" in man is brought about by man's cooperation with the Divine Logos indwelling within man. Deification or divinization is Athanasius' unbiblical way of saying what Irenaeus and the earlier Fathers implied by the process of man's moving from the *image* to the *likeness* of God, as narrated in Genesis 1, 26.

H. Strater summarizes this thought well:

In the very existence of the Man-God, the redivinization of humanity is accomplished in its source. It is in the make-up of the person of Christ that for Athanasius the Redemption has its center of gravity. The fact of the inhabitation of the Logos in humanity has made it possible for humanity to penetrate into the divine life. Such is the fundamental thought of his soteriology in which he evidently depends on St. Irenaeus.[29]

Only if Christ united within Himself both the divine and human natures could divinity overflow to humanity and by its divine forces, heal and immortalize it.

Who will not agree that such a thing is truly divine? For if the works of the Word's Godhead had not taken place through the body, man had not been deified; and again, had not the properties of the flesh been ascribed to the Word, man had not been thoroughly delivered from them. But though they had ceased for a little while, still sin had remained in him and corruption, as was the case with

mankind before Him. . . But now the Word
having become man and having appropriat-
ed what pertains to the flesh, no longer do
these things touch the body, because of
the Word who has come in it, but they
are destroyed by Him, and henceforth men
no longer remain sinners and dead according to their proper affections, but having risen according to the Word's power,
they abide ever immortal and incorruptible.[30]

We note that the Word comes into the human
body; and by His power He effects the change,
giving men that which is proper to God by His
nature, namely, to be immortal and incorruptible.
Christ's activities are viewed exclusively in the area
of restoring us humans to the dignity from which
we fell through sin, namely, sons of God. This is
the sole purpose of the Incarnation, Athanasius tells
us, in this oft-quoted statement:

The Son of God became the Son of Man
in order that the sons of men, the sons of
Adam, might be made sons of God. The
Word, who was begotten of the Father in
heaven in an ineffable, inexplicable, incomprehensible and eternal manner, came
to this earth to be born in time of the
Virgin Mary, Mother of God, in order that
they who were born of earth might be
born again of God, in heaven . . . He has
bestowed upon us the first-fruits of the
Holy Spirit, so that we may all become sons of God in imitation of the
Son of God. Thus He, the true and natural
Son of God, bears us all in Himself, so
that we may all bear in ourselves the only
God.[31]

If we were to examine further St. Athanasius'
work against the Arians, we would find constantly

his doctrine of the divinization of the faithful spelled out whereby they are adopted into the sonship of God and deified through the grace given them by Jesus Christ the Word.

It can safely be stated that before Athanasius, no Father had taught with his insistence and clarity the physical concept of man's divinization through Christ. It becomes for Athanasius the vertebrae of a theological system of the Trinity's relationships to man. By becoming divinized, man enters into a similar relationship to the Father as that which obtains between the Father and the Heavenly Son. This relational sonship is given man by the God-Man through His physical presence living within man and through the operations of the Holy Spirit making man continually by participation more into what the Divine Son is by nature—the Son of the Father.

THE OPERATION OF THE HOLY SPIRIT

In his apologetic tracts against the heathens and in defence of the divinity of Christ in His Incarnation, Athanasius usually points out the role of the Incarnate Logos in effecting man's divinization.[32] But it is in his four letters to Serapion against the heretical *Pneumatomachoi* who denied the divinity of the Holy Spirit that Athanasius employs a similar argument, used by him before to prove the divinity of the Logos, but now to defend the divinity of the Holy Spirit. Both the Arians and the *Pneumatomachoi* recognized that the Holy Spirit had a role to play in our divinization. Athanasius' argument runs simply: that, if the Holy Spirit effects man's participation of the divine nature, the Spirit cannot be a created being to bring about such an effect that is above all creatures. The Spirit must be God.

Athanasius' basic argument throughout his constant use of the image doctrine is that which even the heretics agreed on, namely, that all sanctification "comes from the Father through the Son in the Holy Spirit."[33] Again he says simply as a universal principle that apparently was accepted by all, including the heretics: "Nothing can become which does not become or is done except through the Logos in the Spirit."[34]

Again in the same letter[35] he calls the Holy Spirit the chrismation or ointment and seal. The Logos anoints and imprints upon man His seal which is the Holy Spirit. More precisely, the Holy Spirit performs in man's divinization a role similar to that performed in the Incarnation. The Logos assumed a human nature through the action of the Holy Spirit:

> When the Logos descended into the Holy Virgin Mary, the Spirit came at the same time into her and in the Spirit it is that the Logos was formed and His body was adapted, wishing through Him to unite and offer the Creation to the Father.[36]

Trying to prove the divinity of the Holy Spirit Athanasius clearly points out from the Spirit's divinization of creatures that He is above creatures. Since the Logos was united to a human nature by the Holy Spirit, it is logical to believe that the whole of humanity would be united to the Logos through the same Holy Spirit.

> It is then in the Spirit that the Logos glorifies Creation and deifies it and adopts and conducts it to the Father. But He who unites Creation to the Logos would not make part of the created world just as He who confers filiation upon creatures would not be a stranger to being a Son. If such would be the case, one must search for another Spirit because in the first Spirit man is united to the Logos. This, however,

is absurd. The Spirit does not make part of created things, but is proper to the divinity of the Father and it is in Him that the Logos deifies the creatures.[37]

Father Régis Bernard offers an interesting sidelight in Athanasius' doctrine of image.[38] As the Logos is the Image of the Father and man is made "according to the Image" that is Christ, Athanasius makes the Holy Spirit the Image of the Son and through the Spirit man is made *kat'eikona*. These texts can be found in the first and fourth letters of Serapion:

> The Son is in the Spirit and in His own Image just as the Father is in the Son.[39]
> The Spirit has been called and is really the Image of the Son . . . Since therefore they (the heretics, especially the Pneumatomachoi) hold that the Son is not a creature; His image cannot either be a creature. For, as such is the Image, so such must necessarily be He of Whom He is the Image.[40]
> It is clear that He is not a creature who is not absolutely of the nature of angels who are fallible, but who is the Image of the Son and He the Image of the Father.[41]
> The Son is the Image of the invisible God and the Spirit is the Image of the Son.[42]

The heretics opposed Athanasius' statements that made the Holy Spirit the Image of the Son by maintaining that such a relation of the Holy Spirit to the Logos would make the first either the Son of the Son or at least a brother with Him of the one Father.[43] But Athanasius insists from the scriptural statement that the Holy Spirit is the stamp or seal of perfection that the Spirit in regard to man completes and perfects the work begun by the Logos.

The Son condescends to the imperfect, but the Holy Spirit is the seal of the perfect.[44]

MAN'S COOPERATION

Although the divinization or perfection of the *kat'eikona* of man is brought about as a gift given *in radice* by the Father in creation and completed through the Son in the Holy Spirit,[45] man, nonetheless, must cooperate in this process. In his main works, Athanasius rarely descends to this level to point out man's role. Usually his image doctrine, as presented above, is connected intimately with his anthropology and man's relation, more precisely, to the Logos or ultimately to the Trinity. To complement the theoretical dogmatic teaching of Athanasius, we must turn to his main ascetical work on the Life of St. Antony. In his *Vita Antonii*, that holds a unique place in the history of Christian asceticism and monasticism, Athanasius, without ever referring directly to his image doctrine, in substance, outlines what serious Christians do to live "according to the Image." In many passages Athanasius attributes the process of man's sanctification to the divine operations of God within the individual.[46] Typical of this synergy of man's cooperative action with that of God is the following text:

Truly the Lord worked with this man—He who for our sakes took on flesh and gave to His body victory over the devil. Thus all who fight in earnest can say 'Not I, but the Grace of God with me.'[47]

Still there are other passages that could indicate a Pelagian attitude towards man's perfection, namely, that man by sheer dint of will power could overtake and possess the kingdom of Heaven. In viewing such texts one should keep ever in mind the audience for which Athanasius intended this work. He was

106

trying precisely to stimulate already generous souls with greater service to God. Thus the accent is placed on man's will power in wanting to cooperate with God; yet that God begins the process and continually directs it both Athanasius and his readers never for a moment lost sight of. A passage such as the following could in itself convey the wrong interpretation:

> When you hear virtue mentioned, do not be afraid of it nor treat it as a foreign word. Really, it is not far from us; no, the thing is within us, and its accomplishment is easy if we but have the will.[48]

For the proper understanding of such a passage one must interpret it in the light of Athanasius' total concept of man's nature. In his very existence man has received a relationship to the Logos that, through deliberate sin or consciously developed virtues modeled on the example of Christ, is lesser or more developed "according to the Image," that is Christ.

> Virtue has need only of our will, since it is within us and springs from us. Virtue exists when the soul keeps in its natural state. It is kept in its natural state when it remains as it came into being. Now it came into being fair and perfectly straight . . . For the soul is said to be straight when its mind is in its natural state as it was created. But when it swerves and is perverted from its natural condition, that is called vice of the soul.[49]

We note in this text that Athanasius tends strongly to equivalate the supernatural life of grace with a growth of union between man's mind and that of God through illumination and knowledge. The principal effect of an increase in grace through the ascetical practice of virtues is that the human intellect (*nous*) be illuminated to "see" God. In this life this vision of infused faith is a pre-matured anticipation of the beatific vision. Jesus Christ is the Image that reveals the Father. This He does by giving to man the *kat'eikona* which is the expanding power, dependent upon our own efforts to cooperate, of knowing God and hence of loving Him.

Athanasius' doctrine of the assimilation of man to the Logos combines in a very balanced way the Alexandrian intellectualism of Clement and Origen without at the same time destroying the dynamic, ontological union with Christ inhabiting the human person through grace, as St. Irenaeus taught. By consistently teaching a determined meaning of *eikon* as applied only to the Divine Son towards the Father and a fixed meaning of *kat'eikona* as that ontological relationship of Christ to the individual man through the Divine Life-Grace, Athanasius places the *image* doctrine on the basis of a principle capable of synthesizing the whole of his theology into a clear unity.

CHAPTER SEVEN
THE CAPPADOCIANS: ST. BASIL THE GREAT AND ST. GREGORY NAZIANZEN

Historians of patristic thought call St. Basil, St. Gregory Nazianzen and St. Gregory of Nyssa the "Great Cappadocians." Diverse in temperaments and talents, these three were intimately united either by the bond of blood brothers, as were Basil and Gregory of Nyssa, or by friendship, as existed among all three. Through their many talents as theological thinkers, preachers, writers, church administrators, these three aided to solidify the teachings of the first two ecumenical councils of Nicaea (325) and Constantinople (383) throughout all of Asia Minor.

In this chapter we wish to present the teaching of St. Basil and St. Gregory Nazianzen on the image and likeness of God in man and to reserve the following entire chapter to the rather full and complex teaching of St. Gregory of Nyssa.

ST. BASIL (c. 330-379)

St. Basil was the eldest of ten children born of a wealthy and solidly Christian family in Casearea of Cappadocia. He was trained in the footsteps of his father who was a very successful rhetorician and lawyer. Basil studied in the classical tradition of his day, first at Caesarea, then Constantinople, the capital of the Byzantine Empire, and finally in Athens. In 356 upon the completion of his studies, he was baptized and visited the monks of the desert in Egypt, Palestine and Mesopotamia. He resolved to become a solitary and settled on the

Iris River. He soon developed a community of monks who were eager to be directed by such a holy, intelligent and prudent person as Basil. His solitude was ended in 370 when he was chosen to be the bishop of Caesarea. For nine years he fought against the Arians and worked valiantly as a pastor to provide spiritual education and the corporal works of mercy to his flock. His writings are numerous and are divided into dogmatic treatises, discourses and homilies (usually preached directly by Basil), ascetical and liturgical works plus a great number of letters.

MAN CREATED TO GOD'S IMAGE

In the writings of St. Basil, strangely to say, there is found relatively little theology of image and likeness. This can be easily understood by the heavily pastoral and biblical emphasis that Basil gives his writings. We will see the opposite in his younger brother, Gregory of Nyssa, who possessed a brilliantly speculative mind and indulged rather freely in using philosophical language not totally found in Holy Scripture.

That this predominant theme of image and likeness of God in man is scriptural is indeed recognized by Basil. We would naturally go to his famous *Hexaemeron*, the nine homilies on the book of Genesis which give a rather literal explanation of the first five days of creation. Here Basil, in dealing with the advent of living creatures, anticipates the doctrine of man made to God's image, but from his stated promise it is clear that Basil also, as all his patristic predecessors, wanted to write a whole treatise on this important subject:

If God permits, we will say later in what way man was created in the image of God, and how he shares this resemblance. Today we say but only one word . . . .[1]

Regretfully Basil never fulfilled his promise, as far as his extant writings show. We do have the "one word" that preceded his promise to develop that more in detail:

> To whom does He say, 'in our image', to whom if it is not to Him who is 'the brightness of His glory and the express image of His person, 'the image of the invisible God'? It is then to His living Image, to Him Who has said, 'I and my Father are one', 'He that has seen me has seen the Father', that God says, 'Let us make man in our image'. Where is the unlikeness in these Beings who have only one image? 'So God created man', it is not 'They made'. Here Scripture avoids the plurality of Persons. After having enlightened the Jew it dissipates the error of the Gentiles in putting itself under the shelter of unity, to make you understand that the Son is with the Father, and guarding you from the danger of polytheism. He created him in the image of God. God still shows us His co-operator, because He does not say, in His image, but in the image of God.[2]

In a moving homily, evidently copied by an auditor as Basil preached his commentary on Psalm 48 to his flock during a liturgical service, we find Basil returning to this picture of Genesis and the image-likeness of God given to man that exalted him over all other living animals. Again, we see no attempt on Basil's part to develop this doctrine through a philosophical anthropology of man. His primary aim is pastoral and he uses the image of God in man to contrast with man's fallen state through personal sin:

> 'Man is a great thing, and pitiful man is something honorable,' (Prov. 20, 6) who

111

has his honor in his natural constitution. For, what other things on earth have been made according to the image of the Creator? To which of the animals that live on the land, or in the water, or in the air, has the rule and power over all things been given? He has fallen a little below the dignity of the angels because of his union with the earthly body . . . But still, the power of understanding and recognizing their own Creator and Maker also belongs to men. 'And he breathed into his nostrils' (Gen. 2, 7), that is to say, He placed in man some share of His own grace, in order that he might recognize likeness through likeness. Nevertheless, being in such great honor because he was created in the image of the Creator, he is honored above the heavens, above the sun, above the choirs of stars. For, which of the heavenly bodies was said to be an image of the most high God? What sort of an image of his Creator does the sun preserve? . . . They possess only inanimate and material bodies that are clearly discernible, but in which nowhere is there a mind, no voluntary motions, no free will . . . .[3]

Thus the distinctive dignity granted both to angels and men of being made according to the image of the Creator consists in "the power of understanding and recognizing their own Creator and Maker." Being like to God, man had the power to recognize this likeness. Still Basil hedges from entering into any speculation as to where this image of God in man is found. In rare places does he condescend to tell us that this image of God in man resides in man's mind. Here we have the image of the Creator.

The mind is a wonderful thing and therein we possess that which is according to the image of the Creator.[4]

All creatures must obey the voice of God the Creator. But man is different as we have seen from Basil's homily on Ps. 48. Man has a special calling which consists in this, that "it is proposed to us to resemble God as far as it is possible to human nature."[5] More precisely, man moves to an assimilation in likeness to God through knowledge which more specifically makes the image of God possible in man.

> You have received an intelligent soul, thanks to which you think about God. You know through the reasoning process the nature of beings and you harvest the most pleasing fruit of wisdom . . . .[6]

But Basil cannot remain long dealing with abstract wisdom or *theoria*. Just as God by His will-act gives reality to creatures and they in turn are subject to His commands, so too God has made man like to Himself insofar as man has a free will to impose his will illumined by reason upon the sub-human cosmos.

> All the early animals, tame or wild, all that live in the waters and those that fly in the air, all are your slaves. They have submitted to your reign. Is it not you who have discovered the arts and constructed cities? All goods which are necessary for you, all which serve you in living better, is it not you who have conceived them? Have you not made the seas accessible through your intelligence? The earth and the waves are they not at the service of your life?[7]

This passage recalls the earlier cited passage from the homily of Ps. 48. God is the Creator and Sovereign of the universe and has made man to

113

His image to participate likewise as a *co-operator* in governing the world. It is not enough, however, that man imposes his will on the brute world around him, but man is obliged by the ontological fact of being made to God's image to exercise his intellect and will in dominating the rest of creation as God does. He who governs the world in the true sense must, like God, be totally free. Although Basil does not treat of man's freedom as often and in the same detail as does St. Gregory of Nyssa,[8] still liberty is one of the indispensable privileges that complement our reason and which constitute the point of similarity or likeness of God in man.

We will see that it is in the area of practical application of a properly formed intellect and will that Basil is more concerned. This is the substance of his ascetical treatises and pastoral homilies: how to develop a proper Christian *gnosis*, a practical knowledge that is a reflection of God's which leads man to execute it by consciously-willed actions.

"There can be no resemblance (to God) without knowledge and knowledge is not had without lessons," insists Basil.[9] This knowledge for Basil is not an academic accumulation of facts about the material universe. The necessary *gnosis* or knowledge wherein the image of God consists is the knowledge of good, the capacity to discern between what is good and what is evil. This clearly presupposes liberty then in order to follow through with the proper execution of doing good and avoiding evil. It consists therefore in knowing which actions can lead man to his happiness and then in freely willing to pursue those actions.

> The soul is freed from every necessity after having received from his Creator the gift of determining his life, since his soul is made to the image of God . . . .[10]

FALLEN MAN

Basil, not only the exegete of Holy Scripture wherein God recounts the history of salvation, but also the practical pastor of souls entrusted to him, knows well the other side of the coin. Possessing a mind that can know good and freely will to do it, man also possesses in that same intellectual freedom "the faculty of turning away from the good."[11] Man cannot accuse God of having acted either unjustly or unwisely in making us free to do good and also evil. To anyone asking: "Why then have we not been created impeccable so that even if man should wish, it still would be impossible for him to sin?" Basil answers:

> Who reproaches the Creator for not having made man impeccable by nature does nothing other than to indicate a preference to be irrational rather than a rational creature, an immobile, inert being, deprived of the ability to be free and active.[12]

But Basil, seeing well that man's wisdom, a participation of God's own knowing and willing, can also be corrupted by error and sin, insists that man's state of being at least capable of constant change does not come from man's intellect and will but rather "from being always in movement."[13] Thus it is not man's liberty or intellect which occasions the fall of man, but it is from his mutability, his fleeting character that the danger of a fall arises:

> But there are in it (the human mind) two faculties; in accordance with the view of us who believe in God, the one evil, that of the demons which draws us on to their own apostasy; and the divine and the good, which brings us to the likeness of God.[14]

In the Greek, Basil uses the word *parapephikasi*, to indicate the important nuance that evil does not come from our nature (*physis*), but is inserted into our nature, however, *para*, that is, against nature's own proper fulfillment. Thus Basil signifies by this word that evil is both in us and is against our true nature. The sin of Adam and the sin of every human being consists fundamentally in man's will, freely choosing evil rather than good. But ultimately what is the explanation why man chooses evil? Basil affirms that "if the soul would remain fixed in contemplating the beauty and would persevere in the joy of the intelligible, it would have the ability and the power to lead a life conformed to its proper nature."[15] Unfortunately, however, man does not continue to live intelligently in keeping with his nature, made to God's image, and then sin results:

> This misfortune happens when through satiety, the soul loses its taste for the blessed delectation. When through a lack of vigilance it grows heavy and falls from the superior regions. It mixes then with the flesh, goaded on by the desire of shameful joys of earthly pleasures.[16]

We can see here the influence of Platonism on Basil's thinking, but more proximately we see the influence of Origen and the neo-Platonic school of Alexandria.[17] The "superior regions" of Origen, however, meant for Basil, following his master's use of the allegory, the concrete creation of man in his perfection with his body and all of the brute world in perfect harmony with man's intellect and will. Basil in speaking of Adam's state before his fall says: "Adam was living previously in the heights, by which expression I understand the thought and not so much a place."[18] The heights are not the stellar world, but the real, concrete world, created good by God. Adam was the image of the perfect man, full of wisdom. There was to be at the beginning a wonderful harmony between

116

the works of God and His Providence on the one hand and on the other the works of man and his wisdom, which was sustained by the continual remembrance of God that manifested itself in praise, service and love.

For the first man the whole of creation was the speech of God externalized. Man listened to creation speak to him of the divine wisdom. But catastrophe soon entered. Adam deliberately allowed himself to look upon the pleasing creatures as charming and agreeable in themselves, for the pleasure they could bring him. He no longer understood the true meaning of creatures in their relationship back to God. To reach this state Adam had to reject from his heart the remembrance of God and in so doing "he filled himself with arrogance and pride." He put himself as the criterion of good and evil; what he wanted was good and what displeased him was evil. His "wisdom" turned to folly. Destined by being made to God's image to share with God in the government of the world, man became by this perverse decision freed from all dependence upon God, the author of a catastrophe that infects the whole of creation.

Origen had depicted sin as the destroyer of the Logos, of the life of Christ, in the human soul, making the sinner *alogikos*, irrational, one who frustrates his rational nature that should find its fullness in a human, intelligent nature but through sin opts to be under the power of the devil, the *alogos*.[19] The image of God for Origen could never be lost by man's sins, but it would be covered over by the "bestial images" which destroy the unity and harmony in man. Basil follows his Alexandrian master, Origen, in this matter by insisting, instead of the image of God remaining after sin, that human wisdom remains and through it the ability to know God somewhat and choose freely the good.

In his *Regulae Brevius Tractatae* (no. 293),

Basil expresses the thought of Origen. Sin imprints on the soul the "image of the devil," the image of the Prince of this world, of Caesar. This tyrant holds the soul captive. Sin would be the complete diversion from God; hence grave, mortal sin would not be one instant act cutting man off from God, but sin would be the final fatal blow placing man under its power.

THE SAVIOR COMES

Basil well describes the state of man in sin with his desperate need for a savior other than himself. He shows how man in sinning threw aside the image of God (God's grace living in man) and put on the "image of the earthly." Yet man's original dignity as a living image of God is made possible through Jesus Christ:

> Man, then, having been advanced above these things in honor, did not understand; he neglected to follow God and to become like his Creator, and, becoming a slave of the passions of the flesh, 'he is compared to senseless beasts, and is become like to them': now he is like an amorous horse which neighs after his neighbor's wife (Jer. 5, 8) . . . Truly there is excessive folly and beastlike lack of reason, that he, made according to the image of the Creator, neither perceives his own constitution from the beginning nor even wishes to understand such great dispensations which were made for his sake, at least, to learn his own dignity from them, but that he is unmindful of the fact that, throwing aside the image of the heavenly, he has taken up the image of the earthly.[20]

Earlier in the same homily, Basil shows how no simple human being could have ransomed his neighbor since no man can persuade the devil to remove from his power him who has once been subject to him.[21] Only Christ, the most perfect man and at the same time God eternal, is capable of redeeming man:

> But one thing was found worth as much as all men together. This was given for the price of ransom for our souls, the holy and highly honored blood of our Lord Jesus Christ, which He poured out for all of us; therefore, we were bought at a great price . . . . No one is sufficient to redeem himself, unless He comes who turns away the captivity of the people, not with ransoms nor gifts as it is written in Isaias, but in His own blood.[22]

Jesus Christ applies redemption to us by sending us the Holy Spirit. But man must use those faculties of intellect and will which contain the root of the image of God in man to repudiate his past sinful actions so as to prepare for justification.

> That we may be justified by the grace of Our Lord Jesus Christ and by the guidance of the Holy Spirit, let us repudiate the customary actions of our own wills and the observance of human traditions. Let us, on the other hand, go forward by means of the Gospel of the Blessed God, Jesus Christ, Our Lord.[23]

The grace of God is absolutely necessary but so also is man's cooperation. Jesus Christ through His sacraments and His living Word of Holy Scripture sends us His Holy Spirit to restore us to our former dignity.

THE WORK OF THE HOLY SPIRIT

Like his contemporary, St. Athanasius, Basil assigns to the Holy Spirit the principal work of restoring man to his former dignity as a son of God. The Holy Spirit is analogous to the form or soul of man's material body. Through the Spirit man is "informed" by a spiritual form, allowing man to perform virtuous acts that he could never perform on his own. In his treatise, *De Spiritu Sancto*, Basil describes the role of the Holy Spirit in restoring the image of God in man:

> Therefore, inasmuch as the Holy Spirit perfects rational beings, completing their excellence, He is analogous to form. For he, who no longer 'lives after the flesh' (Rom. 8, 12), but, being 'led by the Spirit of God' (Rom. 8, 14), is called a Son of God, being 'conformed to the image of the Son of God' (Rom. 8, 29), is described as spiritual.[24]

The Holy Spirit communicates to our intellect a special gift, a force, a new vision, permitting man to overcome his weakness and to penetrate to divine realities. Here we see the ancient principle of psychology at the basis of Basil's thinking, namely, "only like knows like." For Basil it was not enough to possess a spirit or soul, radically similar to God who is pure spirit, but the human soul had to possess a principle of divine illumination living within man.

> As the power of seeing is in the healthy eye, so is the operation of the Spirit in the purified soul. Wherefore also Paul prays for the Ephesians that they may have their 'eyes enlightened' by 'the Spirit of Wisdom' (Eph. 1, 17, 18).[25]

Basil, as Athanasius, worked out the characteristics of the Holy Spirit by outlining the divine activities of the Spirit in the souls of men.[26] The Holy Spirit is the Supplier of life, "omnipresent, the origin of sanctification, light perceptible to the mind, supplying, as it were, through Himself, illumination to every faculty in search for the truth."[27] Since by sin the creature is a slave, it is the Holy Spirit that sets man free. The Spirit gives to the creature life. "The creature needs teaching. It is the Spirit that teaches. The creature is sanctified, it is the Spirit that sanctifies."[28]

The intimate knowledge of God, especially of Jesus Christ who is the Wisdom of His Father, the Image of the invisible God, is communicated by the Holy Spirit. We know the Son through the Holy Spirit or better, as St. Basil himself notes: "It is not said in fact 'through the Spirit' but 'in the Spirit.' "[29] It is the Holy Spirit who "shows the glory of the only-begotten Son and it is in Him that knowledge of God is given to the true adorers."[30] There can be no restoration of man according to the Image which is Jesus Christ unless through the Holy Spirit that dwells within man:

> For it is impossible to behold the Image of the invisible God except by the enlightenment of the Spirit and impracticable for him to fix his gaze on the Image to dissever the light from the Image, because the cause of vision is of necessity seen at the same time as the visible objects. Thus fitly and consistently do we behold the 'brightness of the glory' of God by means of the illumination of the Spirit and by means of the 'Express Image' we are led up to Him of whom He is the Express Image and Seal, graven to the like.[31]

Thus it is the abiding presence of the Holy Spirit within man that effects the sanctification and deification of man. Still the presence of the Spirit is distinguished by Basil from His activities and gifts such as the illumination, the restoration of the Image, the sanctification of man into a living son of God. These operations of the Holy Spirit are purely gratuitous gifts of God's condescending love. Still the Holy Spirit works in man to the degree that man purifies himself through asceticism.

THE WORKS OF MAN

Often it has been leveled against Eastern Christian spirituality that it tends towards passivity. Except for a tinge of Messalianism which is the closest counterpart in the East to the Western Pelagianism, the predominant emphasis, at least to the Western mind, is stressing almost exclusively the action of God, especially of the Holy Spirit, in effecting man's sanctification. In their doctrine of *synergism*, the Greek Fathers maintained a balance that preserved the reality and the mystery between God's activity and man's cooperation. It is Basil above all the other Greek Fathers who formulated a system of asceticism into an organized spirituality of man's works, preparatory to the activities of the Holy Spirit. We can only refer to some of the recent works that have treated the asceticism of St. Basil and outline the general areas that St. Basil touched in describing man's role in cooperating with the Holy Spirit to restore the Logos-Image in man.[32]

As has been pointed out, Basil's purpose in writing was primarily pastoral. He becomes apologetic only in an effort as a pastor to defend his flock against the heretics, especially the Arians. Thus he presupposes, much more than he develops, the traditional themes among the Greek Fathers of divinization[33] and its allied doctrine of image and likeness.

His originality lies in his prudent and practical

judgement of the ascetical means needed by man to attain sanctity. These consisted primarily in a return to God through a *metanoia* or conversion of heart by fear of God, humility and a renouncement of all inordinate desires and passions. These were to be accomplished through silence, flight from the vanishing pleasures and values of the world, poverty and detachment, prayer, reception of sacraments, fasting, control of the thoughts, practice of all the *commandments* of Christ, through virtuous living and, finally, constant practice of charity towards God and one's neighbor for love of God.

At first view St. Basil seems relatively unimportant in the history of the image and likeness doctrine. Still, because of his rigorous practicality, he has bequeathed to the whole of Christianity, of his day and of all times, a richness of teaching on the ascetical practices without which God in His decree of salvation does not work to restore His divine image in man.

ST. GREGORY OF NAZIANZUS

St. Gregory of Nazianzus was the intimate, life-time friend of St. Basil. Unlike Basil, however, Gregory seemed to collapse before the conflicts of everyday reality and was constantly fleeing to solitude to escape the intrigues of men. Yet his native powers as an orator and his zeal for souls, mingled perhaps with a bit of vanity, as von Campenhausen suggests,[33] called him back to take up ecclesiastical positions for which he was not fitted by nature or temperament. He was a powerful orator and poet, sensitive to the praises and criticisms of others. He had the same Hellenic education as Basil, but, where Basil strove for simplicity of expression in order to be understood by all, Gregory displayed a too ornate, classical style of writing that tended to be exaggerated and affected. Still, his keen and delicate mind gave him a rare ability of expressing in short and concise formulas the most abstruse Trinitarian and Christological truths. His writings, mostly discourses, poems and letters, made him the favorite theologian among readers of the Byzantine period.

IMAGE DOCTRINE

Gregory is not a theologian who can be said to have developed a theology of the image-likeness doctrine. Like Basil, he did not write a special work on this subject but he used this concept in the traditional patristic manner of speaking of man's divinization.[34] Because of his penchant for Plato and Plotinus, he was drawn very much to imitate the neo-Platonic Christian writers like Clement of Alexandria and Origen.

Clement had written about the tradition already existing among "Christian philosophers," those "who spoke as Plato, that man received in birth the privilege of being 'according to the image' of God (*kat'-eikona*) and that later man was to attain the likeness of God (*homoiosis*)."[35] Origen, as we have earlier seen, taught also a distinction between image and likeness.[36]

But Gregory links up the double aspect of image and likeness into one formula that becomes his usual expression. An example of this is found in his funeral oration in honor of his sister, Gorgonia:

> . . . her nobility consisted in the preservation of the image and the perfect likeness to the Archetype, which is produced by reason and virtue and pure desire, ever more and more conforming, in things pertaining to God; to those truly initiated into the heavenly mysteries . . . .[37]

Gregory sees the whole dignity of man in guarding this God-given image and likeness to the Archetype. One's nobility is measured by how one has "guarded this (divine Image in man) through virtue and consent to his Archetype."[38] But more precisely the image of God in man is found in man's intellectual soul. In a passage that exhibits Gregory's oratorical powers and was intended by Gregory as a loose commentary on the Genesis account of God's creation of man, he says:

> Now the Creator-Word, determining . . . to produce a single living being out of both the visible and invisible creations, fashions man; and taking a body from already existing matter and placing in it a Breath taken from Himself (Gen. 2, 7) which the Word knew to be an intelligent soul and the Image of God, as a sort of second world. He placed him, great in littleness (a microcosm) on the earth; a new Angel, a mingled worshipper, fully initiated into the visible creation, but only partially into the intellectual; King of all upon earth, but subject to the King above; earthly and heavenly; temporal and yet immortal; visible and yet intellectual; half-way between greatness and lowliness; in one person combining spirit and flesh; spirit, because of the favor bestowed on him; flesh, because of the height to which he had been raised; the one that he might continue to live and praise his Benefactor, the other that he might suffer, and by suffering, be put in remembrance and corrected if he became proud of his greatness.[39]

The "flesh is much inferior to that which is 'according to the image,' "[40] namely, the soul. We carry "the image of the sovereign God"[41] in our souls. The soul is divine and incorruptible because it is a "breath of God."[42]

Henri Pinault has well demonstrated the influence of Plato's writings on Gregory's theology, especially in his doctrine of man's resemblance to God.[43] Gregory uses step by step the same metaphor employed by Plato of the Divine Good as the sun of the intellectual world. To see objects, argue both Plato and Gregory, the organ of sight must become in some way similar to the objects seen. The eye could never see the sun unless it became somehow a form similar to the sun (*ilioeides*). If the mind wishes to perceive the Good, it must open itself to the light of this intellectual sun.

But Gregory goes beyond the speculation of Plato by means of his Christian revelation as a guide to posit a truer view of the return of the image found in man. This return back to its Model does not, however, cause the two subjects, man and God, to be assimilated into the Divine, as Plotinus proposed.

> What God is in nature and essence no man
> ever yet has discovered or can discover . . .
> In my opinion it will be discovered when
> that within us which is godlike and divine,
> I mean our mind and reason, shall have
> mingled with its Like and the image shall
> have ascended to the Archetype, of which
> it has now the desire. And this I think
> is the solution of that vexed problem as to
> 'We shall know even as we are known.'[44]

Gregory speaks of the "test" and the "fall" whereby man was banished from paradise and from God and man put on the "tunics of skin." The temptation was, so Gregory speculates, in the area of contemplation, which was a degree of assimilation to God that man unjustly wanted to anticipate:

> Also God gave him a Law, as a material
> for his free will to act upon. This Law
> was a commandment as to what plants
> he might partake of, which one he might

not touch. This latter was the Tree of Knowledge; not, however, because it was evil from the beginning when planted! nor was it forbidden because God grudged it to us . . . But it would have been good if partaken of at the proper time, for the tree was, according to my theory, Contemplation, upon which it is only safe for those who have reached maturity of habit to enter; but which is not good for those who are still somewhat simple and greedy in their habit . . . but when man . . . forgot the commandment . . . he put on the coats of skins . . . that is, perhaps, the coarser flesh, both mortal and contradictory . . . Yet here too he makes a gain, namely death and the cutting off of sin, in order that evil may not be immortal. Thus his punishment is changed into a mercy; for it is in mercy, I am persuaded, that God inflicts punishment.[45]

Having yielded to this premature desire to possess God by man's own efforts, man was separated from the life of God. He needed a remedy sent by God.

THE LOGOS OF THE FATHER
AS REMEDY

Gregory traces through the whole of the history of salvation, showing the inadequacy of the means which God provided man as medicinal remedies to call the creature back to the Creator. The word, the law, the prophets, threats, plagues, wars, diseases and so forth, all failed to bring man back to God:

As these required a greater aid, so also they obtained a greater. And that was that the Word of God himself . . . Who is before

127

all worlds, the Invisible, the Incomprehensible, the Bodiless, the Beginning of being, light of light, source of life and immortality, the image of the archetypal beauty, the immovable seal, the unchangeable image, the Father's definition and Word . . . came to His own image, and took on Him flesh for the sake of our flesh, and mingled himself with an intelligent soul for my soul's sake, purifying like by like; and in all points except sin was made man. What is this mystery that is around me? I had a share in the image; I did not keep it. He partakes of my flesh that he may both save the image and make the flesh immortal. He communicates a second union far more marvelous than the first, inasmuch as then He imparted the better nature, whereas now Himself partakes of the worse. This is more godlike than the former action, this is loftier in the eyes of all men of understanding.[46]

We see here the basic principle that St. Gregory used against Apollonarius who held that Christ had a defective human nature, not possessing the full human reasoning powers. This principle the subsequent Holy Fathers would repeat constantly: "What is not assumed by Christ is not saved; that alone is saved which is united with God."[47] Precisely because the Divine Logos was a perfect human being was it made possible through His humanity for the Divine Logos to make contact with other human beings and thus bring redemption to individuals. Gregory's writings, especially his sermons and poems, are characterized by vigorous, forceful language to express the reality of the incorporation of the individual through a most personal, intimate union with Christ. The events of Christ's life on this earth, His activities, His miracles are being renewed in our souls. The Passion of Christ is taking place today. He is suffering today in the sense that His members are suffering with Him, He sustaining them by His Divine Life.

> Yesterday I was crucified with Him; to-day I am glorified with Him; yesterday I was buried with Him; today I am quickened with Him; yesterday I was buried with Him; today I rise with Him . . . Let us offer ourselves, the possession most precious to God, and most fitting; let us give back to the Image what is made after the Image. Let us recognize our dignity; let us honor our Archetype; let us know the power of the mystery and for what Christ died. Let us become like Christ, since Christ became like us. Let us become God's for His sake since He for ours became Man.[48]

The redeeming work of Christ in the world begins in the depths of my person: in Christ's transformation of me into a son of God. Thus the Incarnation and Redemption are dynamically viewed not simply as historical events in time and space but Christ's activities going on in an event here and now in the interior life of the individual person as He renews the face of the earth. An *I-Thou* relation with Christ is established through His living presence within the individual soul. To live with Christ is to act as a new creature with Him.

> I must be buried with Christ, arise with Christ, be joint heir with Christ, become the son of God, yea, God Himself . . . This is the purpose for us of God, who for us was made man and became poor to raise our flesh and recover His image and remodel man that we might all be made one in Christ who was perfectly made in all of us all that He Himself is . . . that we may bear in ourselves only the stamp

of God, by whom and for whom we were
made and have so far received our form
and model from Him that we are recognized by it alone.[49]

The image of Christ is "recovered" in us by
our activities "with" Christ. Then finally, after
man has relived, or better, after Christ has relived
His mysteries again in us individually, this is the
vision that Gregory holds out to us as our final
fulfillment:

Lastly, be crucified and share His death
and burial gladly that thou mayest rise
with Him and be glorified with Him and
reign with Him.[50]

Participating in the Second Adam, Christ, we
are divinized already in part and fully only after
death when we will achieve union with Him in
heaven. Man must enter, therefore, into Christ in
this life by putting on the vision of life that Christ
in His humanity possessed. Man must see this
material world, above all the reality of suffering,
with now a partial and eventually a full resurrection, from Christ's view.

THE BREATH OF THE HOLY SPIRIT

It is the Holy Spirit that effects in man this
intellectual vision "according to the Image," that
is Jesus Christ. As St. Athanasius did, so, likewise,
St. Gregory argues to the divinity of the Holy
Spirit by His divinization of man:

I dare to utter something, O Trinity; and
may pardon be granted to my folly, for
the risk is to my soul. I too am an Image of
God, of the heavenly glory, though I be
placed on earth. I cannot believe that I
am saved by one who is my equal. If the
Holy Spirit is not God, let him first be

made God, and then let him deify me his
equal . . . Why do you grudge me a complete regeneration? Why do you make
me, who am the temple of the Holy Spirit
as of God, the habitation of a creature?
Why do you honor part of what belongs
to me, and dishonor part, judging falsely
of the Godhead, to cut me off from the
Gift, or rather to cut me in two by the
Gift? Either honor the whole or dishonor
the whole, o new theologian.[51]

The deification of man, conceived by St. Gregory as a restoration to the divine resemblance, is
connected with a very special presence of the Holy
Spirit within man. Man prepares himself for the
coming of the Spirit through performing the traditional ascetical practices proposed and practised by
the early Church. But it is eventually the Holy
Spirit who illuminates us to put on the "mind of
Christ." In a beautiful passage of counter-pointing
Gregory depicts the role of the Holy Spirit in divinizing man:

He is called the Spirit of God, the Spirit of
Christ, the Mind of Christ, the Spirit of
the Lord and Himself, the Lord, the Spirit
of adoption, of truth, of liberty; the Spirit
of wisdom, of understanding, of counsel,
of might, of knowledge, of godliness, of
the fear of God. For He is the Maker of
all these, filling all with His essence,
containing all things, filling the world in
His essence, yet incapable of being comprehended in His power by the world; good,
upright, princely by nature not by adoption; sanctifying, not sanctified; measur-
ing, not measured; shared, not sharing;
filling, not filled; containing, not contained; inherited, glorified, reckoned with
the Father and the Son; held out as a

threat; the finger of God; fire like God; to manifest, as I take it, His consubstantiality; the Creator-Spirit who by Baptism and by resurrection creates anew; the Spirit that knows all things, that teaches, that blows where and to what extent He wishes; that guides, talks, sends forth, separates, is angry or tempted; that reveals, illumines, quickens or rather is the very Light and Life; that makes temples, that deifies; that perfects so as even to anticipate Baptism, yet after Baptism to be sought as a separate gift; that does all things that God does . . . and making all things clear and plain; of independent power, unchangeable, almighty, all-seeing, penetrating all spirits that are intelligent, pure, most subtle . . . .[52]

Thus we see that, even though St. Gregory of Nazianzus did not work out as clear a theology of image as did St. Athanasius, St. Gregory of Nyssa and St. Cyril of Alexandria, he did give expression to the traditional doctrine of image and likeness, but expressed in Platonic and Neo-Platonic concepts that conveyed a vibrancy in man's personal relations with the three Divine Persons of the Blessed Trinity. A consciousness of man's personal relations with the Trinity living within him moved man gradually from a partial vision of God, strengthened by faith and ascetical works, especially by the frequent and fervent reception of the sacraments, to a full vision of assimilation realized only fully in the Beatific Vision.

CHAPTER EIGHT
ST. GREGORY OF NYSSA

Of the three Cappadocian Fathers, St. Gregory of Nyssa (+c394) brings to his writings a greater speculative mind, enforced with an exact, encyclopedic knowledge of the sciences of his day. He was a thinker, a philosopher and had a talent for systematizing abstract thought. He drew heavily upon Platonic and Stoic writers and was an ardent disciple of Origen, except for the latter's extreme form of *apokatastasis*. A basic emphasis in all his writings is an insistence on the transcendent majesty of God, His unapproachableness by man on his own power, yet the constant revelation of God through Jesus Christ, the perfect Image who reveals the Father to us through the interiority of His divine life within us. An example of his mystical, apophatic spirituality that had great influence on Pseudo-Dionysius and eventually the great mystics of the West is the following passage from his *Life of Moses*:

> True knowledge for the one that is searching is to understand that to see consists in not seeing because He transcends all knowledge by being separated from all parts through His incomprehensibility as by a darkness. This is why John the Mystic (John the Evangelist), who had penetrated into this 'luminous darkness' says that 'no one has ever seen God', defining through this negation that the knowledge of the divine nature is inaccessible, not only to man but to every intellectual nature. This is why Moses, when he had progressed in *gnosis* declares that he sees God in the darkness, i.e. he knows that God is essenti-

ally He who transcends all knowledge and
is outside the grasp of the mind.[2]

To understand Gregory's doctrine of the image
of God in man we must understand his anthropology
of man. His concept of the nature of man can be
found summarized succinctly in the biblical phrase,
God "made man to His own image and likeness."
Gregory starts with God's view of man from Genesis.
Never leaving this starting point, he does not separate the supernatural in man from the natural.
His idea of nature is quite different from the usual
definition found in Western theology or philosophy.
Jean Danielou describes this latter view as comprising both animal and intellectual life to which the
supernatural life is super-added. For Gregory, Danielou continues, nature comprises both the intellectual
and spiritual life while the animal life is something
that is added to man's nature.[3] It would be more
exact to say with Roger Leys, S. J.,[4] that nature in
Gregory's understanding must not be conceived as
either comprising the supernatural life or the animal
life, but, rather, that man's nature is situated in
embryonic form with a directional "pull" towards
one or the other. In his work, *Contra Eunomium*,
Gregory uses the word *methorias*, meaning, *between the two*; that is, man receives in creation a
radical orientation towards both the supernatural
life and the animal life which in the first case is
actuated through the influence of divine grace and
man's constant, virtuous cooperation; in the second
case the animal life is actuated by man's free option
of choosing the things of the flesh over the things
of the spirit.

Thus Gregory conceives the nature of man as
the state of man in *toto* as he was created in
God's concrete plan. He objects to pagan writers,
especially the Stoics, who magnify man because he
is a microcosm composed of the same elements as
the material universe.[6] Man's greatness is not in

a likeness to the created world, but in being according to the image of his own Creator.

God is in His own nature all that which our mind can conceive of good; rather, transcending all good that we can conceive or comprehend. He creates man for no other reason than that He is good; and being such, and having this as His reason for entering upon the creation of our nature, He would not exhibit the power of His goodness in an imperfect form, giving our nature some one of the things at His disposal, and grudging it a share in another; but the perfect form of goodness is here to be seen by His both bringing man into being from nothing, and fully supplying him with all good gifts . . . What difference then do we discern between the Divine and that which has been made like to the Divine? We find it in the fact that the former is uncreated, while the latter has its being from creation; and this distinction of property brings with it a train of other properties; for it is very certainly acknowledged that the uncreated nature is immutable, and always remains the same, while the created nature cannot exist without change; for its very passage from non-existence to existence is a certain motion and change of the non-existent transmuted by the Divine purpose into being.[7]

Here we are brought at once to two common meanings that Gregory assigns to the word, *nature*, (*physis*) which Danielou has clearly pointed out, namely, the use of the word *nature* to refer to God's uncreated being and, secondly, *nature* as applied in the abstract to refer to man's creaturehood as distinct from God's divine life.[8] A third usage, not precisely found in the above text, refers to human nature considered universally in its regenerated state.[9] In the first two usages we can conclude that Gregory does hold a clear distinction between nature and grace expressed usually as an opposition of the created and finite to the Uncreated and the Infinite (God).[10] In the third meaning of nature we see more clearly Gregory's concept of nature in relation to the image of God. This is man as he was first created by God with all the gifts that we consider as supernatural. These gifts include "all virtue and wisdom and every higher thing that we conceive"[11] together with all the gifts of soul and body. In a word, what is meant by man's created nature is the perfection of an integral human nature. Having lost by personal sins these gifts that were as the fulfillment or fruition of the image of God in man, man's nature can only be thus conceived again in his reintegrated or regenerated state. Man's full nature demands the possession of God's life and a participation in His qualities through reflected human virtues. Thus man's nature and its faculties of body and soul that remain after sin are conceived as incomplete until they can be completed by what we call the supernatural.

This is an implied distinction between nature and grace, but the latter is considered not as separated from man's nature but as its fulfillment. M. Lot-Borodine has used the felicitous phrase *fin surnaturellement naturelle* to describe man's nature as image of God (more specifically man's mind or *nous*) oriented not by essence but through a gratuitous finality on the part of the Creator towards its divinized fullness.[12]

PRIMORDIAL IMAGE OF GOD

Nature as used by Gregory in this last sense is nature restored or nature fulfilled. Here we have a return to the full image of God that was given to the first man in creation. But even though sin stripped man of the gifts that had rendered him complete as God had originally conceived him, still man possessed in his nature a primordial image of God that not even sin could destroy. This root-image of God in man Gregory clearly denies to be found in man's body. Here we see Gregory a faithful son to the spiritualism inherited from the Alexandrian school of Philo and Neo-Platonism.[13] It is not in man's resemblance to the created world insofar as he has a material body like other animals but in his elevation to the level of image of the Creator.

This level of the image of the Creator is to be found in man's spirit, the *nous*. Divinity is above all matter and is essentially mind (*nous*) and word (*logos*):

> The Godhead is mind and word; for 'in the beginning was the Word' (Jn. 1, 1); and the followers of Paul 'have the mind of Christ' which 'speaks' in them (1 Cor. 2, 16; 11 Cor. 13, 3); but humanity too is not far removed from these; you see in yourself word and understanding (*logos, nous*), an imitation of the very Mind and Word. Again, God is love and the fount of love; for this the great John declares that 'love is of God', and 'God is love' (1 Jn. 4, 7, 8); the Fashioner of our nature has made this to be our feature too; for 'hereby', He says, 'shall all men know that you are my disciples, if you love one another.' Thus, if this be absent, the whole stamp of the likeness is transformed. The Deity beholds and hears all things and searches all things out; you too have the power of apprehension of things by means of sight and hearing and the understanding that

inquires into things and searches them out.[14]

Leys well points out that Gregory uses *nous* and *logos* synonomously as an hendiadys to convey our concept of *reason*, that critical faculty in man which searches for a synthesis and assures man of dominion over the earth.[15] But Gregory means much more, as the above quotation clearly shows. Man in his intellect and the faculty of love, his will, is made to God's image insofar as man with his highest faculties opens himself "to behold and to hear" God. God is mirrored forth in His image in man through contemplation. Man's *nous* or *logos* is capable of being divinized by its openness to the Divine Logos.

This is one of the most consistent points found among the Greek Fathers in their development of the image doctrine; namely, that man is radically through his intellect and will made "according to the Image of God" who is the Divine Logos, Jesus Christ. In imitation of Christ through faith and the other Christlike virtues, man becomes *logosized*, to coin a word that conveys the precise doctrine of Clement, Origen and Athanasius, to quote only three who developed a rather complete doctrine of the Logos in relation to man.

The proper exercise of man's free will gives to man also a primordial image and likeness to God. Through his free will man can choose to love God and thus be assimilated to a participation of God's nature. It is precisely because man is free that he is like God who is beyond all coercion and restraint in His activities. This is brought out clearly by Gregory in the following text:

> For He who made man for the participation of His own peculiar good and incorporated in him the instincts for all that was excellent, in order that his desire might be carried forward by a corresponding move-

ment in each case to its like, would never have deprived him of that most excellent and precious of all goods; I mean the gift implied in being his own master and having a free will. For if necessity in any way was the master of the life of man, the 'image' would have been falsified in that particular part by being estranged, owing to this unlikeness to its archetype. How can that nature which is under a yoke of bondage to any kind of necessity be called an image of a Master Being? Was it not, then, most right that that which is in every detail made like the Divine should possess in its nature a self-ruling and independent principle, such as to enable the participation of good to be the reward of its virtue?[16]

The closing part of this text shows us that Gregory rightly taught that it is the free will of man that loses the full image by sin and through God's help regains it.

We can therefore readily accept Gregory's equivalating the image of God with man's love for God, since this is merely rephrasing the above text concerning the free will of man as the faculty of choosing God rather than sin. This love comes from God as a gratuitous, infused gift. It is the perfection of all virtues that when attained in its purity brings to man all the other virtues. Thus if faith and the other virtues assimilate man to God, surely love, the perfection of all virtues, is that gift of God restored to man that effects in us the full image of God. This Gregory brings out in his treatise on the soul and the resurrection:

> For this is what love is: the inherent affection towards a chosen object. When, then, the soul, having become simple and

single in form and so perfectly godlike, finds that perfectly simple and immaterial good which is really worth enthusiasm and love, it attaches itself to it and blends with it by means of the movement and activity of love, fashioning itself according to that which is continually finding and grasping. Becoming by this assimilation to the Good all that the nature of that which it participates is, the soul will consequently, owing to there being no lack of any good in that thing itself in which it participates, be itself also in no lack of anything, and so will expel from within the activity and the habit of desire; for this arises only when the thing missed is not found . . . Love, therefore, is the foremost of all excellent achievements and the first of the commandments of the law. If ever the soul reach this goal, it will be in no need of anything else; it will embrace that plenitude of things which are, whereby alone it seems in any way to preserve within itself the stamp of God's actual blessedness. For the life of the Supreme Being is love, seeing that the Beautiful is necessarily lovable to those who recognize it.[17]

Another quality that Gregory uses to indicate the image of God in man is that of immortality. This is more than the natural immortality of the human soul as Socrates proposed in the *Phaedo*, but it refers to the immortality that comes to man through the gratuitous gift of God's own participated life. Immortality and incorruptibility were the two main characteristics that the Greek Fathers spoke about to indicate the distinctive qualities due only to God in His essence. Only God was immortal and unchangeable by His essence, freed from any mutation or movement, from imperfection to a new state of higher perfection. Danielou summarizes well the thought of Gregory in writing:

There is not a question of the natural condition of the incorruptible soul to which the divine life later would be added. There is question only of the ontological, true state, that of man deified who is made incorruptible (*aphthartos*) and the state of the corrupted (*phthartos*), where man is not physically corrupted but is engulfed by corruptible beings around him. It is this positive corruption that is meant. The term *athanasia* (immortality) which we find together with the word *aphtharsia* (incorruptibility) to designate the state of 'image' . . . . calls for similar remarks. The opposition is not between existence and non-being since we are on the human level in which the spirit possesses a radical immortality, but rather between the state of mortality, that is to say, the condition of man separated from God which is true death and, as a consequence of this, is endowed with an animal nature subject to mortality, and the state of *athanasia* (immortality) which is at the same time the life of the soul united to God and the liberation from biological mortality.[18]

It will suffice to quote only one text of Gregory to illustrate how he linked the quality of immortality as a gratuitous gift given in grace by God whereby man would approximate and resemble God, immortal and incorruptible by nature.

Since, then, one of the excellences connected with the Divine nature is also eternal existence, it was altogether needful that the equipment of our nature should not be without the further gift of this attribute, but should have in itself the immortal, that by its inherent faculty it might both recognize what is above it, and be possessed with a desire for the divine and eternal life. In truth this has been shown in the comprehensive utterance of one expression in the description of the cosmogony, where it is said that man was made 'in the image of God.'[19]

THE ETERNAL NOW

One of the interesting areas of Gregory's doctrine on image that has particular appeal to Christion evolutionists, such as E. Messenger,[20] concerns his views on the whole of humanity bearing a resemblance to God's image. Gregory conceives the will act of God's mind as already creating man to His image. In the divine foreknowledge the image of God in man is one that applies to the whole of humanity. In Gregory's view of creation there was an identity between this initial idea and the final fulfillment of that idea through the slow unfolding in time and space, beginning with creation and ending with the *pleroma* attained in the Parousia at the end of time. God's knowledge and power and the actual realization of His idea through His creation and completion of the cosmos are seen by Gregory as all inter-dependent and not to be separrated in their essential reality, although in the actualization there enters the seeming separation (due to finite time and material process) from potency to fulfillment. In his treatise on the making of man Gregory thus expresses his idea:

In saying that 'God created man' the text indicates by the indefinite character of the term all mankind; for was not Adam here named together with the creation as the history tells us in what follows? For here the name given is not the particular but the general one. Hence by the universal term of the nature, we are led to some such view as this: that in the Divine foreknowledge and power, all mankind was included in the first constitution . . . I think that the entire plenitude of humanity was included by the God of all, by His power of foreknowledge, as it were in one body, and that this is what the text teaches us which says, 'God created man, in the image of God created He him'. For the image is not in part of our nature, nor is the grace in any one of the things found in that nature, but this power extends equally to all the race; and a sign of this is that mind is implanted alike in all. For all have the power of understanding and deliberating and of all else whereby the Divine nature finds its image in that which was made according to it. The man that was manifested at the first creation of the world and he that shall be after the consummation of all, are alike; they equally bear in themselves the Divine image.[21]

In Chapter 22 Gregory continues his argumentation from the Genesis text to insist that the image of God is in the entire human nature and had its consummation (or reality) even before Adam, the first man, existed:

I take up once more in my argument our first text. God says, 'Let us make man in our image, after our likeness, and God created man, in the image of God created He him.' Accordingly, the image of God which we behold in all human nature had its consummation then, but Adam as yet was not.[22]

143

In the eternal eye of God, the whole process of man and the universe moving to its *pleroma* or fulfillment is already attained. The image of God in man is both at one and the same time in God's mind and universally and concretely realized. This is brought out by Gregory in his commentary on the opening words of Genesis, where he explains that the Hebrew phrase *be-reshit* which is commonly translated into Greek by *en arche* (in the beginning) is translated in the Aquila Greek recension by *enkephalaio* (in the total ensemble):

> For by 'in the summing up' it is shown that all things were made together, and 'in the beginning' indicates the instant and simultaneity . . . . The commencement of this cosmogony teaches that the sources, causes and powers of all things were collectively sent forth in an instant and in this first impulse of the Divine Will the essences of all things assembled together, heaven, ether, star, fire, air, sea, earth, animal, plant, all beheld by the eye of God and manifest by the word of Power, as the prophecy says, 'He sees all things before their genesis.' But through the Power and Wisdom together sent forth for the perfecting of each of the parts of the world, there followed a certain necessary series according to a certain order . . . appearing not by a kind of automatic chance according to an unordered and fortuitous movement but just as the necessary arrangement of nature required succession in the things coming into being, so each one is said to have come about . . . .[23]

Thus we see that Gregory does not separate the two realities, the commands of God and the works that flow out through God's creative activities into final completion. This dynamic concept of the created world as a concrete totality both in God's mind and in its gradual fulfillment will be used by St. Gregory in his soteriology and recapitulation of humanity by a physical (through grace) incorporation into Christ. It is the whole community of mankind that needs universal salvation. The image of God in man will be precisely the true, fulfilled humanity, which image will reach its perfection only at the end of time with the fulfillment of the eternal decree.

SEX

But before we see the full restoration of the image of humanity by the perfect Image, Jesus Christ, according to whom all humans have been created, it would be profitable to see Gregory's doctrine of sex in relation to man, as image of God. Precisely, Gregory argues, the perfect image cannot be based on distinctions and differences which are at the root of sex. In God there is no distinction of sex; how then can sex be a part of the image? Gregory answers by his theory of a double creation:

> 'God created man,' it (Genesis) says; 'in the image of God created He him.' There is an end of the creation of that which was made 'in the image'; then it resumes the account of creation and says, 'male and female created He them.' . . . Thus the creation of our nature is in a sense two-fold: one made like to God; one divided according to this distinction.[24]

In Chapter 17 also, Gregory concludes that the distinction into male and female does not belong to the image of God in man since our Lord promises that after the resurrection, when the fullness of the image will have been attained, there will be neither marrying nor giving in marriage:

145

For the grace we look for is a certain return to the first life, bringing back again to Paradise him who was cast out from it. If then the life of those restored is closely related to that of the angels, it is clear that the life before the transgression was a kind of angelic life, and hence also our return to the ancient condition of our life is compared to the angels.[25]

Gregory however sees the difficulty that might be concluded from the above texts: that sex was a result of sin. He shows how sex was from the very beginning an essential part of man's makeup. God added the distinction of sex to human nature when in His prescience He foresaw what was going to happen. Sex was given as a means whereby man could make the choices in loving submission to God, and thus through virtuous living according to the mind of God he would be restored to the former state of incorruptibility.

Hans von Balthasar provides us with an insight into Gregory's thought on sex in relation to God's eternal plan, yet in nowise does he give us a sufficient solution to the apparent conflict between the two distinct levels of God's eternal order and the temporal growing into the fullness (*pleroma*) of that order through materiality existing and being perfected in a time-sequence. Von Balthasar maintains that sex for Gregory, along with the human passions, even death, is at the same time a punishment and a blessing. In one sense they are *kata physin*, according to man's nature in the real order, and in another sense, in the ideal order, they are *para physin*, against nature.[26]

Sex and human passions von Balthasar compares to Israel's kingdom. It was at the same time a punishment from God and a gift. God saw that the Israelites would transgress His ideal order so in this sense God permitted the institution of kings as a punishment. It was also an institution that God willed as a means to restore the Chosen People to His love and thus it was according to God's will in the concrete, real order. God, forseeing man's wilful sinning, preordained sex and materiality, mutability and corruptibility as a means by which man would be able through free cooperation to attain the perfection that God had ideally planned for man.

GARMENT OF SKIN

Man is, thus, no longer the perfect, full image of God. To express this state of reality, the created order of man immersed in matter, Gregory resorts to his favorite image from Genesis 3, 21 of the garment of skin. He does not follow Origen's simplistic interpretation of the garment of skin as the body added secondarily to the first preexistent human soul. Gregory uses this rich concept to imply all that comprises mortality and corruptibility as opposed to man's true destiny (both in God's ideal order and in the finally realized order) of immortality and incorruptibility.

Man's present condition is the result of sin, but the garment of skin was actually created by God as the very remedy for sin, given to man even before he sinned, but rendered worse by sin. It is precisely man's mortal state that gives him the very means by which man can, with God's help, overcome evil and regain the original state of immortality and incorruptibility. This is brought out in a passage in Gregory's *Oratio catechetica magna*:

> One who regards only the dissolution of the body is greatly disturbed and makes it a hardship that this life of ours should be dissolved by death; it is, he says, the extremity of evil that our being should be

quenched by this condition of mortality. Let him, then, observe through this gloomy prospect the excess of the divine benevolence . . . Now since by a motion of our self-will we contracted a fellowship with evil . . . falling away from that blessedness which is involved in the thought of passionlessness, we have been viciously transformed—for this reason, man, like some earthen potsherd, is resolved again into the dust of the ground, in order to secure that he may part with the soul which he has now contracted, and that he may, through the resurrection, be reformed anew after the original pattern; at least if in this life he has preserved what belongs to that image.[27]

Gregory seems to imply that the mortal, material element of man, in which part the passions and sex are radicated, was an addition to the intended nature of man. "The grace of the resurrection is the restoration of fallen man to his primitive state."[28] Yet in other places, as has been already suggested, Gregory considers the material body, distinguished by being of one or the other sex, as God's fully willed and created man, through His foreknowledge of man's sins:

But as He perceived in our created nature the bias towards evil, and the fact that after its voluntary fall from equality with the angels it would acquire a fellowship with the lower nature, He mingled, for this reason, with His own image, an element of the irrational . . . .[29]

God's plan provided that man, with a mutable nature, would cooperate in his own liberation. But this process of "return" to man's ideal situation of immortality and incorruptibility was not entirely within man's own power.

CHRIST, THE PERFECT MAN

To overcome the state of human mortality, man needed a being greater than man's own finite, imperfect being.

Now the removal of what is foreign is a return to what is connatural and fitting; and this we can only achieve by becoming what we once were in the beginning when we were created. Yet to achieve this likeness to God is not within our power nor within any human capacity. It is a gift of God's bounty, for He directly bestowed this divine likeness on our human nature at its creation.[30]

Gregory poses the question by whom man was to be restored:

By whom was man to be recalled to the grace of his original state? To whom belonged the restoration of the fallen one, the recovery of the lost, the leading back of the wandered by the hand? To whom else than entirely to Him Who is the Lord of his nature? For Him only who at the first had given the life was it possible, or fitting, to recover it when lost. This is what we are taught and learn from the Revelation of the truth, that God in the beginning made man and saved him when he had fallen.[31]

Following the consistent tradition of all of the Greek Fathers before him, Gregory links up the restoration of God's divine life in man as the primary purpose of the Incarnation:

. . . He was transfused throughout our nature, in order that our nature might by this transfusion of the Divine become itself divine, rescued as it was from death

and put beyond the reach of the caprice
of the antagonist.[32]

Gregory views man's redemption more along
the lines of Origen's *apokatastasis* or restoration of
man by Christ to his fullness rather than along
juridical terms of the repayment by Christ's death
on the Cross of a debt contracted by man's sins.
Christ is pictured as the Good Shepherd, carrying
in His arms the wounded sheep which is the entire
human race.[33] But not content to be the Shepherd,
Christ becomes also "one of the sheep through the
nature that He assumed while remaining the Shepherd through the nature that did the assuming."
Christ is humanity divinized; perfect man, the
model that the Heavenly Father had in mind according to which He created man. Not only by His
example of a perfect life held out for Christian imitation but by His resurrectional life, Jesus Christ
lives in the universe and is effecting the return to or
fulfillment of men according to His own image. The
process of deification of man by the resurrected
Christ begins in Baptism whereby a *koinonia*, a community, is established between the resurrected Christ
and the newly resurrected (spiritually, unto God's
life) human being:

> But the descent into the water and the
> triune immersion of the person in it in-
> volved another mystery. For since the
> method of our salvation was made effec-
> tual not so much by His precepts in the
> way of teaching as by the deeds of Him
> who has realized an actual fellowship with
> man and has effected life as a living fact,
> so that by means of the flesh which He
> has assumed and at the same time deified,
> everything kindred and related may be
> saved along with it, it was necessary that
> some means should be devised by which
> there might be, in the baptismal process,

150

a kind of affinity and likeness between him who follows and Him who leads the way.[35]

Baptism effects this union, but then the mystery of Baptism must be a way of life. That which it symbolizes it also effects in our daily life whereby we are called upon to die to self and rise to Christ through a constant imitation of Him.

> Needful, therefore, is it to see what features are to be observed in the Author of our life, in order that the imitation on the part of those that follow may be regulated, as the Apostle says, after the pattern of the Captain of our salvation. . . . It is imperative on all those who have an equally earnest desire for the Good as He has, to be followers by the path of an exact imitation of Him who leads the way to salvation and to carry into action what He has shown them . . . . The labyrinth of this our life cannot be threaded by the faculties of human nature unless a man pursues that same path as He did who, though once in it, yet gone beyond the difficulties which hemmed Him in.[36]

Gregory shows that Christ subjected Himself to death and to burial in the earth; so too our imitation of Him must be a reenactment of the death of Christ. Jesus in His death united those elements that were separated through sin, namely, soul and body. He effected "this return to union of these severed elements whereby our nature might be purified and obtain freedom from the contamination of any foreign admixture."[37]

Man's imitation of Christ in His resurrection consists:

> . . . in effecting the suppression of that admixture of sin, in the figure of mortification that is given by the water, not cer-

151

tainly a complete effacement, but a kind of break in the continuity of the evil, two things concurring to this removal of sin—the penitence of the transgressor and his imitation of the death . . . . By his penitence he advances to a hatred of and averseness from sin and by his death he works out the suppression of the evil.[38]

Penitence and a continued imitation of Christ's death, although not effecting a perfect dying of a kind identical with that of Christ, nevertheless, will lead us back to a state of partial restoration wherein the purified man arrives at *apatheia*, freedom from inordinate passions.

Now, to the pure, freedom from passion is that kindred state, and that in this freedom from passion blessedness consists, admits of no dispute.[39]

Jesus Christ, God become man, who died and lives through His glorious resurrection, makes man like unto Himself, a son of God. "For one who is a man becomes a son of God by being joined to Christ by spiritual generation;—a man puts off himself and puts on the divine nature . . . A man becomes a son of God, receiving what he has not and laying aside what he has."[40]

To allow for continued growth in the new life initiated by Baptism, Jesus Christ instituted the Holy Eucharist as the most perfect means of inserting Himself into the body of believing man. In this most intimate of unions Christ makes man a participator of His own resurrectional incorruptibility. St. Gregory is noted for the dynamism of his sacramental theology and nowhere is this seen better than in the presentation of his Eucharistic theology. In Ch. XXXVII of his *Great Catechism* we see how Gregory develops his doctrine:

Since the human being is a twofold creature, compounded of soul and body, it is necessary that the saved should lay hold of the Author of the new life through both their component parts. The soul, being fused into Him through faith, derives from that the means and occasion of salvation, for the act of union with the life implies a fellowship with the life. But the body comes into fellowship and blending with the Author of our salvation in another way . . . (against the poison introduced into man's body by sin) what then is the remedy to be? Nothing else than that very Body which has been shown to be superior to death . . . As Paul says, a little leaven assimilates to itself the whole lump, so in like manner that body to which immortality has been given it by God, when it is in ours, translates and transmutes the whole into itself.[41]

Stressing the physical aspects of the Divine Bread as the nourishment in building up the newly acquired Divine Life by Baptism and faith, Gregory continues in the same chapter to explore the question: "How can one Body of Christ vivify the whole of mankind?" Christ's human body into which God entered, by eating bread as all human beings, "was in a certain measure the same with it, that nourishment, changing itself into the nature of the body." The same divine power that changed the physical bread that was eaten by Jesus Christ into the Body of God the Word effects a similar change in the Eucharist by changing bread and wine into His Body and Blood. This divine nourishment then effects a change in man, but instead of the consumed food becoming the person consuming, the person is changed into the Divine Food.

. . . since God infused Himself into perishable humanity for this purpose, namely that by this communion with Deity man-

kind might at the same time be deified,
for this end it is that, by dispensation of
His grace, He disseminates Himself in every
believer through that flesh whose substance
comes from bread and wine, blending Himself with the bodies of believers, to secure
that, by this union with the immortal,
man, too, may be a sharer in incorruption.[42]

Not only is the Image of God restored and
made living within man by the fervent reception
of the sacraments, but this process of deification
is effected by man's continued life of prayer and
Christian virtues. Especially in his treatise on *The
Lord's Prayer* does Gregory show the absolute necessity of prayer in order that man can attract the
energizing activity or the grace of God to effect
a continual growth in the likeness of God. Human
nature, once weakened by evil, is incapable of transforming itself or of doing any kind of good.[43] Still
God asks man's cooperation and gives to man the
power to will freely "the choice of the good."

The basic virtues that Gregory stresses in the
restoration of God's image in man are faith and
humility. We have already seen how man is first
united to God in faith and Baptism. This virtue of
faith is infused by God in man's will, yet it flows
over as a supernatural *wisdom*, a way of knowing
God. Experiential knowledge of God by God is preserved from subjectivism on the one hand and sheer
rationalism on the other by maintaining, through
a profound sense of humility, the transcendence of
the almighty God. As a theologian and philosopher
he stops short before the mysteries too deep for
human comprehension. His speculative treatises
abound in expressions similar to the following:

His grace is surely present in those who
are regenerated in this mystical dispensation (Baptism) . . . For that grace is there

is a matter of faith, on account of Him who has promised to give it being Divine.[44] For though we believe, as we do, that all the corporeal and intellectual creation derives its subsistence from the incorporeal and uncreated Being, yet the *whence* and the *how*, these we do not make a matter of examination along with our faith in the thing itself. While we accept the fact, we pass by the manner of the putting together of the universe, as a subject which must not be curiously handled, but one altogether ineffable and inexplicable.[45]

UNION WITH GOD

Fr. Jean Danielou has well described Gregory's stages of higher union between man and God, highlighting especially the apophatic approach so distinctive in Gregory's writings.[46] He offers the capital text in which Gregory describes this interior, infused vision of faith that progresses through stages of darkening as man is rendered incapable of using his own natural powers with an equal illumination by God through His self-revelation.

> True knowledge is to understand that to see is really not to see since He (God) transcends all knowledge, being separated from all parts through His incomprehensibility as by a heavy darkness. This is why John the Mystic (John the Evangelist) who had penetrated into this 'luminous darkness', says that 'No one has ever seen God,' defining through this negation that the knowledge of the divine nature is inaccessible not only to man but to every intelligent nature. This is why Moses when he had progressed in knowledge declares

that he sees God in darkness, that is to say, he knows that God is essentially He who transcends all knowledge and is not grasped by any mind.[47]

Here man's encounter with God is effected in the realm of pure faith and an ever increased withdrawal from any human intellectual activity or support. In this "luminous darkness" man "sees" God and is assimilated to Him in a union of wills. We see Gregory's mystical language in his description of this intimate union between man and God, described as the *aisthisis parousias*, the sentiment or experiential realization of God's presence. The Divine Spouse appears in the darkness of the night of the senses and makes His presence felt with a clear knowledge of the infinite reality, and at the same time this knowledge reveals the reality as always covered or veiled.[48]

As God reveals Himself to the individual soul through a faith that ever grows deeper, the powers of the soul expand and "stretch forth" towards God as the only true object, as the end or image according to which God created man. As the soul approaches God through contemplation, it is filled with an increase of grace or of God's life that assimilates the human soul to God's nature without making it identical to God. Gregory, as Jean Danielou so well points out,[49] develops a mysticism of the soul's "stretching out" towards God that he calls *epectasis*. St. Paul first used the word in his letter to the Philippians: "Brothers, I do not consider that I have reached it. But one thing I do; forgetting what is past, I am one straining (*epekteinomenos*) towards what is ahead."[50] Etymologically the word summarizes according to Danielou the double polarity that forms the basis of Gregory's mysticism. The Greek prefix, *epi*, indicates a grasping, a surrounding of an already possessed good. For Gregory it indicates the deep interiority of

156

the soul turning within to ponder the lineaments and the presence of God living within the soul. The other Greek prefix, *ek*, emphasizes a going-out of self, a hurling of oneself out of one's limited finiteness towards the Infinite God. Here we find the two basic pulls in any truly Christian mysticism—the entry into one's self to find God immanently present and living within us and at the same time a thrust to get out of our own confinement and to lose ourselves in the transcendent Other—God.

Gregory thus adds an extremely dynamic element to the doctrine of image, which includes at one and the same time the immanence of God along with His transcendence, the lineaments already possessed and enjoyed and the goal not yet attained that draws us with increasing generosity and love to a union that will be consummated only in the fullness of Being, God Himself.

The genius of Gregory's mysticism lies in his intermingling of paradoxical elements of change and continuity, of stretching out for the "Unpossessed" at the same time as reposing in the presence of the "Possessed." The spiritual life is presented as a perpetual transformation of the human soul into a progressively greater likeness to Jesus Christ. This progress is described in vivid terms common to any biological process of growth, thirst, hunger, expansion forward, etc. All of Gregory's speculation is guided by the teleology of the final goal—transfiguration into the Image—Jesus Christ. The flowering of the sacramental life, of prayer and of virtue is the restoration of the Image of God which is the attaining of union with God even in this life. Gregory searches for a new image to describe the inner thrust that God has implanted in man's nature towards this union with God and he finds it in the idea of "wings":

> Now with regard to the graces which they
> receive from God who glorifies those who

glorify Him . . . we know that man at his creation in the beginning was made to the *image and likeness* of God. And this was because as an image it was in all things like its archetype. But, according to the Scriptures (Can. 6, 4; Ps. 16, 8; etc.) our prototype has wings. Hence it follows that man's nature was also created with wings, that in this point, too, it might possess the divine likeness. It is clear, of course, that the word "wings" here (Can. 6, 4) will be interpreted on an allegorical level suitable for the divinity. Thus the wings would refer to God's power, His happiness, His incorruptibility, and so on. Now all these attributes were also in man so long as he was still like God. But then it was the inclination towards sin that robbed us of these wings. Once outside the shelter of God's wing, we were also stripped of our wings. Hence "the grace of God hath appeared" to us, enlightening us, "that, denying ungodliness and worldly desires," we might once again grow wings through sanctity and righteousness (Tit. 2, 11 & 12).[51]

We can understand why Gregory is not much concerned to posit a clear distinction between image and likeness, between a natural potency distinct from its supernatural fulfillment. He presents his doctrine of image as a dynamic presentation of grace, conceived as a relationship within a loving community between God and man. In this relationship there is perpetual progress as the soul is constantly being transformed according to the Image of Jesus Christ. Each expansion of the soul prepares it to receive a still greater likeness to Christ. The powers of the soul are unlimited in the degree of mirroring forth the Image of God. In the life of union with God, every end is a new beginning, a further initiation into the process of transformation that in this life knows no static end to the degree of assimilation to the Divine Image. This thought of constant growth spurred on by unquenchable thirst for greater being is described by Gregory in the following passage:

> Thou art always to the same degree higher and loftier than the faculties of those who are rising to Thee . . . Thus the new grace we may obtain is greater than we had before, it does not put a limit on our final goal; rather for those who are rising in perfection, the limit of the good that is attained becomes the beginning of the discovery of higher goods. Thus they never stop rising from one beginning to the next, and the beginning of ever greater grace is never limited.[52]

Because finite man can never perfectly mirror forth the full image of God, man's growth in a greater likeness admits of infinite possibilities. It is to Gregory's credit that he constantly stresses, in presenting his doctrine of God's image in man, the deifying, transformative powers of divinely infused love as the ultimate kernel that constitutes the image of God in man. This love is the permanent element that persists once man has been restored to God's image. Yet, through *desire* which is rooted in faith and hope and assigned to this present life of mutability and change, this love grows until it reaches the fullness of being in the final assimilation to God's divine nature. We can conclude in no better way than by citing Gregory's own words in which he describes in his treatise, *On the Soul and the Resurrection,* the final end when the process of growth and change gives way to eternal bliss:

> Whenever the soul, then, having divested itself of the multifarious emotions, incident

to its nature, gets its Divine Image and, mounting above desire, enters within that towards which it was once incited by that desire, it offers no harbor within itself either for hope or for memory. It holds the object of the one; the other is extruded from the consciousness by the occupation in enjoying all that is good; and thus the soul copies the life that is above and is confirmed to the peculiar features of the Divine nature; none of its habits are left to it except that of love, which clings by natural affinity to the Beautiful. For this is what love is: the inherent affection towards a chosen object. When, then, the soul, having become simple and single in form and so perfectly Godlike, finds that perfectly simple and immaterial good which is really worth enthusiasm and love, it attaches itself to it and blends with it by means of the movement and activity of love, fashioning itself according to that which it is continually finding and grasping. Becoming by this assimilation to the Good all that the nature of that which it participates is, the soul will consequently, owing to there being no lack of any good in that thing itself which it participates, be itself also in no lack of anything, and so will expel from within the activity and the habit of desire: for this arises only when the thing missed is not found. For this teaching we have the authority of God's own Apostle, who announces a subduing and a ceasing of all other activities, even for the good, which are within us, and finds no limit for love alone.[53]

When such, then, have been purged from it (evil) and utterly removed by the healing processes worked out by the fire, then everyone of the things which make up our conception of the good will come to take their place: incorruption, that is, and life, and honor, and grace and glory and everything else that we conjecture is to be seen in God and in His Image, man as he was made.[54]

CHAPTER NINE
ST. CYRIL OF ALEXANDRIA

When Cyril died on June 27, 444, he had seen over sixty years of life. Almost half of that time he lived as patriarch of Alexandria. His own fiery and impatient nature reflected the turbulent theological unrest of the Church as it strove to express in ever more articulate human concepts the ineffable mystery of divinity and humanity meeting in the person of Jesus Christ. It was his Christological terminology that was accepted in the condemnation of Nestorius in the Council of Ephesus (431).

In spite of the great authority which Cyril's theological writings enjoyed in the early Church, he himself would not have considered his works of any great originality. He strove to give the traditional teaching of the "Holy Fathers" that preceded him, and their authority was second to Holy Scripture.[2] St. Cyril's theology would therefore be patristical in the sense that he himself defined it: "To inquire into the beliefs of the Holy Fathers which came about through the inspiration of the Holy Spirit, to keep firmly in mind the train of their thoughts."[3]

Campenhausen nominates Cyril as the first of the Byzantine scholastics.[4] At least, for our purpose, we can be assured that Cyril's teaching is an adequate summation of the best theological traditions of the Eastern Fathers.

Cyril brings Christology to its highest point of articulation in his theological writings against Arius and Nestorius. It is also in the framework of his Christology that we are to find his doctrine concerning the image and likeness of God in man. Nowhere does he work out a consistent theology of image, yet perhaps no Father had done more to

162

formulate the general traditional consensus of the Greek Fathers on this subject than Cyril. More specifically, it is in his treatment of man's sanctification, as both J. Mahé[5] and L. Janssens[6] have pointed out, that we find Cyril's doctrine of image and likeness, although the terms do not occur as often as they do in the writings of his predecessors.

To understand Cyril's concept of man as made to God's image, we must turn to Cyril's short discourse on the various kinds of possible images. Cyril says:

> Therefore the first image is that of a natural identity in like properties as in the case of Abel born of Adam, Isaac of Abraham. Another consists in only the similarity in external features and an exact rendering of the form as a picture of a king done in wood or in any other artistic medium. Then an image can refer to morals and a behavioral conduct of life wherein one strives toward virtue and honesty. Thus an upright man is said to be similar to Paul, a wicked man to Cain. The same striving for virtue or vice thus can be said to be a likeness of one person to another. There is still another type of image which consists in dignity, honor, glory, and excellence if, for example, one succeeds another in a position of command and he should carry out with proper authority everything that his predecessor would have deemed proper. Another image is that which regards a certain quality or quantity possessed by two persons or things; some shape or proportion of things that are generally by their natures like other things.[7]

Cyril gives this general discourse in his commentary on St. John's Gospel only as an introduction to his presentation of how the Son is a natural image of the Father and hence a perfect example of the first type of image. In many other places, especially in his polemical arguments against Arius and Nestorius and the Anthropomorphites, Cyril develops the doctrine of Christ as the perfect image of the Father because of His divine sonship. The Son, by nature, is of the identical nature of His Father. He argues in his *Thesaurus*:

> . . . no creature is naturally and perfectly like to God the Father and, yet, the Son is, since whoever sees Him sees the Father. How, then, can He be a creature who enjoys a perfect and absolute likeness (*homoioteta*) to the Father?[8]

He is the image of the Father by reflecting perfectly the same nature as the Father. The Son can never lose that which He possesses by nature, namely, to be the Son of God the Father. Hence He possesses all the perfections of the Father, being of the same nature.[9] Thus the Son is the natural image, mirroring perfectly the divine nature of the Father. From this Cyril moves to a comparison of man as an image not by nature but by *participation* (*methexis*). No created being could ever be by nature, he argues, of the same nature of God or a perfect image of God, for he would be by nature finite at the same time as he would be infinite; mutable and immutable; imperfect or perfectible and perfect.[10] In saying that man participates in the image of God, Cyril affirms that man's nature is totally other than that of God's.

MAN IS MADE TO GOD'S IMAGE

That man has been made to God's image is a fact that has been universally accepted by all of his patristic predecessors including heretical opponents, so Cyril does not even take the pains to present this assertion in an orderly fashion. He is more concerned with describing wherein this image resides. Following the Alexandrian tradition of Clement, Origen, Athanasius, Basil, Gregory Nazianzen and Gregory of Nyssa, Cyril denies categorically that man mirrors forth God's image in his material body. We can understand Cyril's stress that the soul is the image of God in man in keeping with the intellectualism of the Alexandrian school. Thus the more Semitic approach of Genesis, carried on by the Antiochene school of Irenaeus with the emphasis on the totality of man as a person made to God's image, was lost to him. In refusing the human body any share directly in God's image, Cyril is refuting the crude doctrine of the *Anthropomorphites* who conceived God Himself in the bodily likeness of a man. These two reasons explain, therefore, Cyril's consistent teaching that the image of God in man is found in the human soul to the absolute exclusion of the body. This is clear in the following text:

> Man upon earth, as far as his bodily nature is concerned, is dust and ashes; but he has been honored by God, by having been made in His image and likeness—not in his bodily shape, that is, but rather because he is capable of being just and good, and fitted for all virtue.[11]

Again Cyril exalts the soul over the body and gives as the reason for the soul's dignity the fact that it has been made to the image of God:

> The soul is more noble than the body since it is the image and breath of God. The body however as its instrument cooperates with the soul in any good endeavor. We must have care of both . . . and let us refer the soul through its exercise of virtues back to the cause from which it came, namely, God who created it.[12]

In the same vein, in a letter in which Cyril intends to refute the Anthropomorphites of Egypt who took the account of man's formation in Genesis literally to mean that God has a corporeal body, he insists:

> It is certain and indeed outside of any controversy that man, made to the image (*kat'eikona*) of God, has this likeness (*homoiotis*) which is not corporeal. God is incorporeal, which fact the Savior Himself teaches in saying: 'God is spirit' . . . That man is made to the image of God has another sense and significance. For only He, above all other living beings on earth, endowed with reason, is merciful and capable of acquiring every type of virtue. He also possesses the power over all things on earth according to the image of God by which He has been fashioned.[13]

From this citation we see how Cyril typically interchanges the words, *image* (*eikon*) and *likeness* (*homoiotis* or *homoiosis*). In not making a distinction between image and likeness Cyril is being faithful to his two masters, Athanasius and Gregory of Nyssa, on whom he depends greatly in this matter of image theology.[14]

In presenting his exegesis on Genesis 1, 26, Cyril carries through his consistent synonymous usage of the words, *selem* (image) and *demut* (likeness) to imply no distinction whatsoever.[15] Here Cyril's exegesis of Genesis 1, 26 approximates that of modern exegetes who refuse to see a distinction made by the compiler of the Priestly Tradition. Rather, the Semitic sense is to present *image* and *likeness* as two forms of an hendiadys.[16]

We have already shown that Cyril places the image of God in man's soul. It is "the soul created to God's image"[17] that makes man totally different from all other animals and capable of a radical relationship to God. But if all men have souls from the first moment of their creation and the soul is an essential constitutive component of man, it would seem logical to deduce that therefore in Cyril's thinking, man could never lose the image of God.

In arguing against the Anthropomorphites that the image is not in the body, Cyril makes the point that men do lose the image of God by a life of sin in forsaking the life of virtue.[18] But no man can lose an essential component part of his nature; therefore he concludes that the image cannot be in the body. We could force him to conclude also that *a pari* the image cannot be in the soul either.

Cyril shows in many other texts that the image more precisely is found in man's reason or intelligence. Still the question persists: how can Cyril maintain that man can lose the image of God since man could never lose his essential characteristic as a thinking being? If man's intellect alone has been made according to the image of God, it would seem therefore that for Cyril the image of God in man is a natural gift, bequeathed to every man by reason of creation. How does Cyril's image doctrine provide for God's gratuitous gift of His own life to man with the possibility of man's continued growth in this life by his own cooperation, if the image is merely man's faculty of understanding?

CYRIL'S ANTHROPOLOGY

To answer these questions we must investigate Cyril's anthropology. Although on the one hand he places the image of God in man consistently in the human soul, on the other hand he consistently also maintains that this image can be lost. Cyril insists that original man possessed not only intellect and will as the *radical* image of God but also possessed the very life, the presence of the eternally existing God. God gave man a share in His divine life that Cyril, true to the whole Eastern patristic tradition, summarizes by the quality of *aphtharsia* (incorruptibility). God is incorruptible, hence immutable, immortal, all-perfect, but these qualities flow necessarily from His nature. God must by His nature be incorruptible. Man is created also with this incorruptibility but as a gift that God adds to man's nature; hence incorruptibility or the *being-like-God* gift comes purely gratuitously to man from God. "God has created all things in incorruption" (*aphtharsia*).[19]

God makes man a participator in God's own nature by breathing into his face a breath of life, the Holy Spirit sent by the Son. This divine breath is not the soul which is inamissible but it is the Holy Spirit that the Creator imprints as a reflecting image of Himself on man.

> When Adam in the beginning was created, God gave him a most perfect beauty in so far as He added to that nature a participation of His spirit. 'He breathed into his face the breath of life' (Gen. 2, 7). Truly the living spirit of life is of Christ. When he was stripped through deception in sin, the Spirit also was stripped. However, it was the good will of God the Father to have an over-all plan of all things related to Christ and thus planned the return of man's nature to its ancient beauty. Thus we received through grace that of which the advent of sin stripped us. Christ breathed upon us after His resurrection and renewed us to the ancient beauty of man saying: 'Receive the Holy Spirit . . . .'[20]

Thus we see that man's incorruptibility and immortality depend not from man's nature but from the double communication of the Divine Spirit. The full image of God in man, hence, is that which allows man to be "a living being, truly beautiful and very like God, possessing the imprint of the supreme glory and the image of the Divine Power on earth."[21] Adam possesses the divine image not by merely having a soul, but rather by being a rational being, inclined towards virtue[22] by the living presence of the Holy Spirit within Him. It is the Holy Spirit who forms man through a dynamic growth into a more perfect image of the Creator by means of the virtues within him, through his cooperation with the force of the Holy Spirit living in man.

In summary, therefore, Cyril is telling us that in Adam there was a double image and likeness to God. One was given radically to man insofar as man had a rational intellect that was oriented by its nature to be completed in virtuous living; the other, by far superior to the first and due to the presence of the Holy Spirit living in man, gives to man a participation in the divine nature. Adam was to cooperate with the active presence of the Holy Spirit within him through virtuous actions and thus he was to grow into a greater realized *sonship* to God. Yet Adam disobeyed God and lost the image, the presence of the Holy Spirit. He lost "that splendor which brings to man sanctity and kinship (*oikeiotiti*) with God."[24] Man was stripped of his incorruptibility and all other gifts of God that man did not possess in his essence. "Mortals were made such from a mortal (parent)."[25] Man lost his superior divine likeness or image yet his human nature was preserved intact.[27]

THE ROLE OF CHRIST

Deprived of the image of God by the absence of the Holy Spirit within him, man lost also his sonship to the Father. Alone, corruptible and mortal, man could never on his own recover the life of God for himself. It is Jesus Christ, the only begotten Son of the Father, the perfect image of a Son to His Father, who can fashion man into his original image of a son of God. Upon the dual principle of solidarity and exchange, Cyril constructs a dynamic theology of redemption.

Cyril's basic formulation that presents the raison d'etre of the Incarnation, which he repeats incessantly, can be phrased: "The Son of God became our Brother that in Him and through Him we might become sons of God." This is merely to rephrase the unanimously expressed patristic principle of soteriology that "God became man in order that men might become gods." By emphasizing the exchange-solidarity theme, the sonship-brotherhood frame of reference, Cyril circumvents the juridical concepts of theological manuals and highlights the rich personalistic elements in the Christian doctrine of redemption.

Capitalizing on the paradox contained in the words applied to Christ as both the Only-begotten Son (*monogenes*) and the First-born (*protogenes*), Cyril shows how Christ, the eternal Son, incapable of brothers, through the Incarnation forms a bond of solidarity in brotherhood with all men. We see as a typical example of the development of his thought the following passage of commentary on St. Luke's text: "She brought forth her first born Son" (Lk. 2, 7):

> Though He is the Only-begotten with respect to His divinity, having become our brother now He is also called the First-born, so that just as He has been made the first-fruits of the adoption of men, He might make us also sons of God. Consider that He is called the First-born in regard to the mystery of the economy, for in His

divinity He is the Only-begotten. Again, as the Word of the Father He is Only-begotten having no natural brothers nor any others numbered with Him, for the consubstantial Son of God the Father is one and alone. But He is the First-born because of His condescension towards creatures.[28]

A little further on Cyril specifies the purpose of this condescension that has affiliated Christ with all men as brothers:

He has ever been the Only-begotten by nature . . . but He is the First-born for our sakes, so that because He is called the First-born of all created things, whatever resembles Him may be saved through Him.[29]

More explicitly still he tells us that the First-born Son of the Father became our brother in order that in Him and through Him we might be sons of God by nature and by grace.

For He alone is both the Only-begotten and the First-born; Only-begotten as God; First-born insofar as He became through the salvific union a man among us and among many brothers. By this we also in Him and through Him according to nature and grace have been made sons of God. According to nature insofar as we are one in Him (through the same human nature); by participation and according to grace through Himself in the Spirit.[30]

L. Janssens explains our consubstantiality with Christ through His Incarnation from the principle that generation is proof of numerical unity. Through His human birth Christ is consubstantially one with us and we with Him. The Divine Word had to take flesh in order to be one of us; but once He dwelled in human flesh, He unites Himself to us and us to

Him. From this principle there follow certain onto-logical relations of fraternity with the Son of God and of sonship with the Father. The distance be-tween the Only-begotten Son before His Incarnation and men was too great to speak of fraternity. But when He became man in the flesh, a part of crea-tion, He became a brother of those who are in the same flesh and blood.[31]

This relation of brotherhood leads to a new relation of sonship between all men and God the Father. For this reason did He descend to us, to raise us to participated sonship that was His by nature. Our *radical* similarity to Christ is established by the human condition that He fully assumed:

> The matter is clear, namely, the Word of God the Father was born of a woman ac-cording to the flesh; He who as God was Lord of the Law has been made subject to the Law in order that He might be de-clared the brother of those held fast by the Law's tight fetters: all this, that we might be adopted as sons. For it is certain that if he had not been made subject to the servile Law nor experienced birth from a woman we could not have become His brothers, for He is by nature Lord and God.[32]

The sonship by adoption is more clearly brought out in Cyril's text of commentary on Christ's ascension:

> (He has emptied Himself) for us and for our sakes so that 'found as a man', though still Son in power, He might in the whole-ness of the flesh obey the word: 'Sit thou at my right hand.' Thus, through Himself He may transmit to the entire human race the glory of sonship by adoption . . . . So He has appeared as man before the Father 'on our behalf that He might restore us

to the Father's presence who had been cut off from it by the ancient transgression. He has sat there as Son in order that we, who are like sons, might be designated sons of God through Him. The fact that Christ who sits there is in all things like us, in that He appeared as man (though it is understood that He is God of God), somehow confers on us the grace of this dignity.[33]

But if all men are consubstantially united with Christ after the Incarnation, why is not all of humanity already sanctified?[34] Grace and man's individual cooperation through virtuous living seem superfluous. Cyril foresees the difficulty and hence carefully distinguishes man's sonship *in* Christ from adoptive sonship *through* Christ. All men truly enjoy a radical kinship with God *in* Christ insofar as He, through the Incarnation, has associated us as our Brother, thus creating an orientation of sonship towards the Father. Still he conceives a more immediate ontologically realized relationship of sonship in grace *through* Christ in His physical mediation of the Spirit of adoption. This sonship is given in Baptism and increases in the Eucharist for those who open themselves to Christ in a faithful obedience.[35] Thus the radical sonship of all men to God Cyril calls sonship "by nature." The sonship in grace through Christ he calls sonship "by grace and participation." This double sonship is illustrated in the text quoted above (note 30: *de recta fide ad Theodosium*) where Cyril uses the terms: by nature (*physikos*), by grace (*kata xarin*) and by participation (*methektos*).[36]

In the light of this distinction we can conclude that for Cyril the image of God in man is rooted radically in the human soul, but is concretely realized by the actualized sonship given individual men through Christ in His Spirit of adoption.

Through the grace of adoption we participate in the divinity of Christ, being made "partakers of the divine nature (II Peter, 1, 4) by Christ's Spirit of adoption who is given to us in Baptism through the unique physical mediation of the Incarnate Word. Unlike Moses who was given by God a functional mediation, Jesus Christ in the unity of His person unites both the divine and human nature. He becomes the truly physical point of mediation between man and God. As God, Jesus Christ communicates the Holy Spirit. But in His humanity Christ, as ourselves, needed to receive the Holy Spirit. His human soul never lost the image of God, yet His human soul was not divine by nature, but always human. In this sense His human soul received the Image which was the Only-begotten Son of the Father. In this sense His human soul was sanctified by the gift of the Holy Spirit. Thus, rather than introducing a form of Arian adoptionism, this doctrine leads us to the distinction of the gift of the Holy Spirit *through Christ* in grace given by Himself to His humanity along with the distinction that the Holy Spirit is given to humanity through the physical mediation of Christ as head of the human race.[37]

SANCTIFICATION IN CHRIST

The mediation of Christ that effects an increase in our filiation with the Father brings about also our sanctification. Christ takes the initiative in this process. We are sanctified in Him, the God-Man, who precisely as God can raise us through His Spirit to a participation in the life of the Godhead. This deification or process of developing the image or likeness in man to God's nature is effected through the human nature of Christ who is encountered principally in the sacraments of Baptism and the

Holy Eucharist. This Cyril brings out clearly in two commentaries of the Gospels of John and Matthew:

The Lord has most clearly explained the sense in which we are made one with Him, and making plain the benefit of His teaching, He said: 'I in them and you in Me, that they may be made perfect in unity.' For the Son dwells in us even corporeally, as man commingled and united with us by the Eucharistic Mystery. Moreover, He is in us spiritually, as God, by the power and grace of His Spirit, building up our spirit in newness of life and making us partakers of His divine nature.

Christ, then, is clearly the bond of our unity with God the Father—as Man, He has bound us to Himself, but also to God, inasmuch as He is God inherently. For in no other way could that nature which is subject to corruption be uplifted to incorruption, except by the descent of that Nature which is above all corruption and change, raising to its highest good that which is sunk low, and by communion and commingling of Itself with the condition of created things transforming unto Itself the nature which is in itself completely other.[38]

Taking the chalice the Lord gave thanks, that is, He prayed to the Father as if declaring Him Associate and Collaborator in giving us the life-giving mystery—as well as giving us a pattern of first giving thanks and then breaking and distributing the bread . . . . Most clearly, moreover, He said: "This is my body . . . this is my blood." Lest you think that these things are a figure, rather than that they are

175

truly offered to be transformed by the mysterious power of Almighty God into the body and blood of Christ, having been made partakers of which, we take on the vivifying and sanctifying power of Christ.[39]

Cyril sees the Eucharist as the climaxing point of encountering Christ and of growing in divinization through a physical union with Christ. That this is a physical union and not merely a moral bond of united wills Cyril emphasizes with language that is far from ambiguous:

Through one body, His own, He blesses, by a mysterious communion, those who believe in Him and He makes them concorporeal with Himself and with one another. Who can now separate them or deprive them of their 'physical' union? They have been bound together into unity with Christ by means of His one, holy body. For if we all eat of the one bread we all become one body, since there can be no division in Christ . . . . Since we are all united with the one Christ through His sacred body, and since we all receive Him who is one and indivisible into our own bodies, we ought to look upon our members as belonging to Him rather than to ourselves.[40]

The transforming effects of the Eucharist are further described by Cyril:

If mere contact with the sacred flesh of Jesus gives life to a dead body, should we not experience effects still more wonderful when we receive the sacred Eucharist? Surely it must completely transform those who receive it into its own perfection, i.e. into immortality . . . Corruptible as we are in the flesh, we lost our own weakness

176

by this 'mingling' and we are transformed into what is proper to the Eucharist, that is, into life.[41]

THE HOLY SPIRIT—
PERFECT IMAGE OF THE SON

Like his predecessor, St. Athanasius, from whom Cyril depends greatly,[42] Cyril, although he attributes to the whole Trinity all divine actions *ad extra*,[43] seems, nevertheless, to attribute our sanctification in a special manner to the Holy Spirit.[44] Ignoring our distinction of appropriations or properties attributed to the individual Persons of the Trinity, Cyril views the work of our sanctification through the Holy Spirit in keeping with the Eastern Fathers' view of the Holy Trinity. J. Mahé gives three reasons for Cyril's special assignation of the Holy Spirit in man's divinization:

1. He is the place, the bond of union which binds our souls to the Son and Father.

2. He is the image of the Son; in imprinting Himself on our souls, he refashions them to the image of the Son and consequently to the image of the Father.

3. He is the sanctifying power of the Divinity. Sanctity is as essential to the Holy Spirit as Paternity is to the Father and Filiation is to the Son.[45]

In the following text from the *Thesaurus* Cyril shows that the Holy Spirit is the intermediary, effecting our divinization; and hence indirectly he shows that the Holy Spirit is divine by nature and not like us who are divinized by participation:

It is seemingly useless to admit an intermediary in the sanctification of the creature when the goodness of God does not disdain to come even to the smallest and sanctify them through the Holy Spirit . . . The law of Moses was imperfect but we believe that the grace of Our Lord is true and perfect. What then is this grace if not the infusion of the Holy Spirit into our hearts, according to the word of St. Paul? But how would the grace which is in us be true if sanctification were given to us through a creature? . . . If the Holy Spirit does not work through Himself in us, if He is not by nature that which we know, if, after having been filled by the divine essence of a participated sanctification, He could only commune to us a grace which had been given to Him, it is evident that it is through a creature that the grace of the Holy Spirit is administered to us. But this is not so . . . The Holy Spirit works through Himself in us, truly sanctifying us and uniting us to Himself.[46]

We have already pointed out in the chapter on St. Athanasius that he insists in several clear texts that the Holy Spirit is the perfect Image of the Son.[47] Cyril follows him in this, including the somewhat singular exegesis of St. Athanasius on the text of St. Paul: "For those whom He has foreknown, He has also predestined to be conformed to the image of His Son, so that this Son should be the first-born among many brothers."[48] That the Holy Spirit is the true image of the Son Cyril proves simply by citing Paul's text. Then, having established this identity in nature, he goes on to show that it is the Holy Spirit that makes us true images by participation as He is by nature:

For the animal endowed so commonly by birth would never have portrayed anything like that supreme image except it have been born (undoubtedly by the will of God) unto that formation through the Spirit, as if to a certain most beautiful face. For since the true image of the substance of the Only-begotten is the Spirit, as Paul writes: 'For those whom He foreknew, He predestined to become conformed to the image of His Son.' The Spirit renders those in whom He exists conformed to the image of the Father, that is, to the Son. And so He recalls all things through the Son to Him from whom He is, the Father, through the Spirit. He requests that the nature of man be renewed and reformed in a certain way conformable to that first image through participation of the Spirit, as it was clothed with that first grace. When the likeness has been recovered, we shall be found stronger and braver than sin which rules in this world, and we may adhere to that only love towards God. When we are fastened interiorly to all good and have overcome the desire of the flesh, we shall behold the unchangeable dignity of the image fixed in us. For this is the spiritual life, this is the power and the nature of worship in the Spirit.[49]

Cyril's theology of grace and the image of God in man are well summarized in a dialogue in his treatise on the Trinity in which he insists that the Holy Spirit, the perfect image of the Son, restores the original image of God in man through His indwelling presence. We see how Cyril insists that it is the substantial Person of the Holy Spirit and not a mere created grace that sanctifies man:

A. Is it not the Holy Spirit who imprints in us the divine image and after the manner of a stamp communicates the supernatural beauty?

B. Very well, the adversaries answer; but

179

He does it not because He is God but only as a minister of the divine grace.

A. Then, it is not He but a grace conferred through Him which is imprinted on us?

B. Yes, so it seems.

A. But then we must call man an image of grace, rather than an image of God . . . And yet it is a truth that our soul is regenerated only in receiving the image of God.

B. Without a doubt.

A. But if the grace, conferred by the Holy Spirit, is something separated from His essence, why did not blessed Moses say clearly that the Creator, after having given existence to the first man, breathed into him grace? And why did not Christ say: 'Receive the grace through the instrumentality of the Holy Spirit'? Moses said 'the breath of life' for the divine nature is a true life because it is in it that we live and move and have our being. The Savior says: 'The Holy Spirit' and it is this Spirit who introduces Him and makes Him inhabit our souls. Through Him and in Him, He leads our nature back to its primitive state, that is to say, refashions us to His own proper likeness through sanctification . . . . The Spirit is the perfect and natural image of the Son. Having been formed according to this Spirit through sanctification, we put on the form of God. It is this that the Apostle (Paul) tells us: 'My children for whom I am in labor until Christ be formed in you.' Christ is formed in us through the Holy Spirit who refashions us according to God . . . The Holy Spirit is then God who remakes in us the image of God, not through any instrumental grace, but in giving Himself as a participation of the divine nature to those who are worthy.

B. I have nothing against what you have said.

A. But we are called and really are temples of God and gods. But why? Our adversaries explain it that we receive only a simple grace and not a grace of the Divine Hypostasis. But it is not so. We are temples of the Spirit, really subsistent, and we are called gods because of Him since through our union with Him we are in communication with the divine nature . . . . The Holy Spirit is then not different from God in substance.[50]

Therefore, Christ, the perfect image of the Father, is formed in us by the Holy Spirit who fashions us in an ever increasing likeness to Christ. In a final text to illustrate the role of the Holy Spirit in effecting our sanctification Cyril explains how the Spirit remakes man to God's image:

Surely the Holy Spirit does not paint the divine essence in us like a scene-painter with Himself something other than it. It is not in this way that He brings us to God's likeness. Rather, being Himself God and proceeding from God, He is Himself impressed invisibly in the hearts of those who receive Him, like a seal in wax. Through communion and likeness to Himself He paints our nature completely to the archetypal beauty and makes man once again to God's image. How, then, will He be a creature, He through whom our nature is reshaped to God, inasmuch as it is made partaker of God.[51]

Cyril continually emphasizes that it is personal holiness which leads us to divinization. Thus the full image of God in man is realized only in the eternal life. This acquired divine life in man does not change man's nature, making him a new god by essence, but, retaining his full human nature, man participates in the divine life that admits of no limit in assimilation. Yet in the process of assimilation neither man's nature nor that of God's is changed into the other. The Holy Spirit makes us pass to another state of existence, yet we are always fully human.[52] To understand Cyril's final point concerning God's image in man, we must see how he conceived the glorified or deified man.

MAN IN PARADISE

The transforming activity of the Triune God inhabiting the human soul thus transfigures man's nature without changing it. Cyril's thought now and again admits of a distinction between the presence of the uncreated Trinity within man and the resulting transformation. The latter is amissible and can grow.[53] Although the effect, man's deification according to the image that is Christ, is distinct from the cause, namely, the Triune activity in man; nevertheless, Cyril would never claim that the two can ever be separated in man.[54]

Even in this life the transforming activity of God brings with it many prerogatives and privileges which only in the resurrected, final life will be received by man in their fullness and will then be inamissible. A special beauty is given to man, placing him not only in dignity above all other creatures but giving him a dominance over the cosmic creation that God had originally bequeathed to Adam. The first man was created by God as His image. "God molded an image, made it a rational animal and, that it might rise above its own natural essence, He immediately imprinted on it the incorruptible, life-giving Spirit . . . Man was the impress of the supreme glory and the image upon earth of the divine power."[55]

Man concretely manifested the image of God by showing forth a similar power of dominance that God possesses over all creatures. The command that God gave the first man over the lower creatures is a consequence of the engraven image of God in man. Adam (and his progeny was supposed to have followed him in this) was made to the Creator's image and was appointed to rule over the things of the earth.[56] But sin destroyed the image of God in man along with the prerogative of dominion over other creatures. Jesus Christ restores, through His Holy Spirit, the image and brings back to man a share in God's dominance over the created world. But only in the full future life of Heaven will this dominance be complete.[57]

Another prerogative enjoyed even in this life through the possession of the image of God but only fully after our resurrection is that of incorruptibility. Because we possess God's life in our souls, we also are incorruptible. Here we see Cyril equating both material and spiritual corruptibility to the wages of sin, while incorruptibility flows to man's body as well as his soul as a gift accompanying the Triune inhabitation in man. This new life that comes to us through the reforming of God's image is a life proportioned to God's nature which is by essence incorruptible and immortal. This newly acquired divine life is more than the mere natural incorruptibility and immortality of the human soul. We remain men, yet we are made that which we are not by nature, namely, incorruptible and imperishable:

> Our transformation will not be a transfer into some other nature . . . for we shall be what we are, that is, men—but we shall be incomparably better. The point is this,

183

we shall be incorruptible and imperishable, and besides this we shall have been glorified.[58]

This incorruptibility is linked directly by Cyril to our redemption. In the following rather long but central text we see Cyril approaching the purpose of Christ's Incarnation, not as directly as we have above so often quoted, namely, to make us gods by divinizing us into participators of His nature, but rather with the intent to give us incorruptibility. Thus we see how intimately Cyril, as all of his patristic predecessors did, linked the prerogative of incorruptibility and immortality with man's newly divinized state:

> The Creator devised as it were a second root of our race, to bring us back to our former incorruptibility, in order that, just as the image of the first man, the man from the earth, engraved on us the necessity of dying and involved us in the meshes of corruption, so, conversely, the second beginning, the one after Him, that is, Christ, and the likeness to Him through the Spirit, would stamp us with indestructibility, and just as disobedience subjected us to punishment in the former, so in the latter compliance and complete obedience might make us partakers of the blessings from heaven and the Father . . . The Only-begotten Word of God came down among us of His own accord, not to have death rule over Him as well as over us, as though Adam transmitted death to Him as well; for He it is who gives life to all. His purpose was to show our form held fast by corruption and transform it into life . . . For it would be absurd to think that Adam, who was earthborn and a man, could send hurtling into the whole race,

184

like some inheritance, the power of the curse that was leveled at him, while Emmanuel, who is from above, from heaven, God by nature, did not give on His part a rich participation in His own life to those who might elect to share His kinship through faith.[59]

We see, therefore, how the concept of incorruptibility for Cyril is a prerogative that flows from the restored image of God in man and hence Cyril uses it freely as a synonym for the renewed image. Incorruptibility is for Cyril the added life of God that elevates the natural incorruptibility of man's soul to a participation in God's own life.

But the ultimate reason that Cyril gives to justify the newly acquired beauty and dignity in man, restored to God's image through the grace of God's life living within man along with the dominance over nature and a participated incorruptibility similar to God's, is because man has become a true son of God. This is the keynote to Cyril's image and likeness doctrine and it highlights the mediation of the God-man in the process of restoring and bringing to completion the image of God in man.

But they who mount to God's adoptive sonship by faith in Christ are baptized not into some created being but into the Holy Trinity itself through the mediation of the Word, who links what is human to Himself through the flesh which is united to Him, and who is linked naturally to the Father inasmuch as He is God by nature. This is how the slave rises to sonship: through the sharing in the true Son he is called, and as it were, ascends, to the dignity that belongs by nature to Him. That is why we are called, and are, begotten by God; through faith we have received the regeneration that comes through the Spirit.[60]

It is by reason of our divine filiation as sons of God that we are thus made to the image of Christ, the perfect image of His Father and hence we are rendered immortal and incorruptible. In our final resurrection those of us who die in the state of sonship of God will not die eschatologically. The saved "will participate in the life and glory of Christ for He will transform the body of our humility in rendering it conformed to His glorious body."[61]

CHAPTER TEN
A PATRISTIC ANTHROPOLOGY

Much more could be added to these preceding chapters through an investigation of the image-likeness theme in the writings of the Fathers of the Desert, of Methodius Olympus, Didymus the Blind, John Chrysostom, Pseudo-Dionysius, Maximus the Confessor, John Damascene, Symeon the New Theologian, Gregory Palamas and the modern Orthodox writer, Serge Bulgakov. But the golden period of patristic speculative theology closes with St. Cyril of Alexandria who forms the final "seal of the Fathers."[1]

We have seen the fluidity with which the Greek Fathers employed the biblical structure of image and likeness. Only a study of each individual Father was able to yield something of the special, rich nuances intended by the ancient witnesses to the Christian message of man's divinization through the Divine Logos. It would be well, by way of summary, to bring together some of the common insights into the patristic anthropology that stem from the image-likeness doctrine, keeping in mind, however, the warning that the Fathers were aware of having used the image-likeness structure, not in any strictly moulded form imposed equally on all writers employing this structure, but of having a liberty to use it in a flexible variety of meanings, depending on the individual's purpose in a given writing.

IMAGE AND LIKENESS

If man has been made by God to His image and likeness, where in man, according to the early Fathers, are the image and likeness found? Is the image of God in man different from the likeness? Even before the fourth century there had arisen a plethora of opinions, as our study has indicated, that prompted St. Epiphanius to refute them as being false or incomplete and finally to say impatiently: "Where the image is and in what part it consists, God alone knows. But we should admit the image in man, lest we appear to reject God's gifts and refuse to believe Him."[2] After having examined the individual writings of the early Greek Fathers on their doctrine of image and likeness, we quite understand Epiphanius' impatience. Even Irenaeus, who clearly distinguishes between image and likeness in many texts, much more clearly than do Origen and Gregory of Nyssa, in other contexts seem to deny the distinction.[3] His predominant teaching, however, presents man, created by nature according to God's image, insofar as he possesses a spiritual soul that partakes of the immortality of God. This *imago in plasmate*, present in the historical creation of each individual human being, is set upon a dynamic road that leads progressively to a higher ontological likeness to God made possible by divine grace. No one can ever lose the first image; the second, the *similitudo per spiritum*, likeness through the Spirit, can be lost, as in the case of Adam, through sin. Athanasius, Basil, Gregory of Nazianzus, and Cyril of Alexandria followed Irenaeus in his distinction of an image by nature and a likeness through grace.[4]

The Alexandrian school, launched into image-theology by Clement and Origen, preferred less an ontological distinction than a dynamic progression in the moral order. Man's image of God by nature, his intellect and will, were perfectible through a life of virtue, modeled on the perfect Image of the Father, the Logos. St. Gregory of Nyssa and St. John Chrysostom follow the Alexandrians in lessening the distinction between natural and supernatural, nature and grace and, as moralists, appeal to their listeners and readers in an effort to move their wills to embrace a life of imitation of Christ-like virtues which in turn are the fruit of the seeds planted in the natural image, the intellect and will of man.[5] Especially for Gregory of Nyssa, similitude or likeness to God (*homoiosis*) is the progressive realization of the image; it looks to the future of man's virtuous striving to rediscover in its first purity the divine image according to which man has been created, but which has been soiled and disfigured, though not destroyed by sin.[6]

These two views of image and likeness are in no way contradictory. Only by consulting the individual Fathers in order to see in what context were they using these two concepts can we see their difference of emphasis yet harmonious teaching in regard to man's ontological nature as it came from God. We can see what happened to that nature through sin, and what through man's free cooperation and God's gratuity of grace can result at the end of a progressively more perfect life of imitation of Christ.

Using as background this general doctrine of the Fathers, that is, the image of God as being man's intellectual nature containing the faculty whereby man can be responsive to God's invitation, and the divine likeness as the progressive movement towards the state or end of the divine elevation of man's nature to the true sonship of God, we can try to work out a theological anthropology of the Eastern Fathers in an attempt to see especially how nature (*physis*) and grace (*charis*) are related in Greek patristic thinking. In Father de Lubac's much discussed book, *Surnaturel*, he seeks to show that the early Fathers, with their dynamic approach based, not on any possible *natura pura* or even *natura integra*, but solely on the concrete, historical human nature, never admitted a nature that was not at the same time by its very ontological makeup, coming from the hand of God, dynamically in movement towards its supernatural end.[7] It would be wrong to assert that the Fathers denied the possibility of a pure nature, a human nature not having God as its final end. The Greek Fathers never thought of the problem. Not faced with the Pelagian heresy, as St. Augustine was who bequeathed his important and subtle distinctions to Western theology, the Greek Fathers viewed the inter-relationship of nature and grace in terms of one continuous unfolding process of two different but not contradictory entities: man's ontological nature and God's gratuitous gift of grace that drew out of the image a more perfect similitude to the perfect Image of God, the Divine Logos. What was the common understanding of the Fathers when they used the word *physis* or nature? The oppositional characterization of nature and grace as found in the Imitation of Christ, Book III, Ch. LIV and LV, where nature is depicted as being corrupt, tending always to vice while grace is the elevating, infused force that allows the spiritual man to do good, would never have come from the pen of an Eastern Father. Fundamentally, nature for the Fathers is the *opus Dei*, as it comes from the hand of God. This work of God, as Irenaeus, Origen and Gregory of Nyssa repeat constantly, is good, and in this initial creation, as man comes forth from God, man finds his dignity and value in the sight of God, and his reason for hoping in the goodness of God. For the Fathers, God did not create a nature without also creating for it an end towards which nature tended, and only in the beatific vision would the restoration be complete. Then, not only the individual soul but all creation would reach its *apokatastasis* or reintegration in Christ.

The whole man, body, soul and superior faculty, intellect (*nous*), was created good. The whole scope of the spiritual life is nothing more than to restore nature to its pristine state of perfection as it came from God. In the Western concept of man's nature, man has animal and intellectual life; through a supernatural elevation (above nature), therefore added to nature (*hyper physin*), man's nature becomes changed. It now assumes a different life, that of grace, which makes man's nature, now infused by grace and elevated above his *natural* nature, completely different than it ontologically was before.

In an earlier chapter it was indicated that St. Gregory Nyssa (and in this his influence has been the greatest of all Eastern spiritual writers) had never distinguished between the intellectual life and the supernatural as two separated levels of man's activities. These two realities, the *nous* (intellect) and the *pneuma* (spirit), constitute for Gregory man's nature insofar as these possess the faculties of knowledge and will by which man can determine himself freely to be responsive to God's "energies" working within man's being. The animal life, *psyche*, although it was created good by God, nevertheless contained the seeds of distension, multiplicity, and materiality leading away from man's fullness into incompleteness, disorder and sin.[8]

Thus we can say that for the Oriental Fathers nature was considered in the historical sence as embracing all that Adam had from God (and all that was good) before sin. Every possible good that is inherent in nature or could come to nature (e.g. in the Western concept of infused grace) is considered as *kata physin*, or in accordance with nature. *Hyper physin* or "above nature" (in the Western concept of the supernatural) was used very rarely among the Eastern Fathers.[9] *Hyper physin* has the ordinary meaning of something extraordinary, exceptional. Grace, being something good, had to be *kata physin*, in keeping with nature.

Other attributes of the anthropology of man's nature from God before sin entered are free will and the patristic concept of free determination. One cannot understand the anthropology of man's nature after sin unless this concept of free will is first understood. God made man's nature free, endowing it with two attributes. *Autexousion* (from *autos*: means *oneself, itself* and from *exestin*: means it is *possible, permissible*) implies that man of his own power is free from any internal force or obligating necessity. No outside force, distinct from man's free will, not even God, can force man to violate his will, to go against his own will. This means that only man himself determines himself. This does not mean that man, in giving his free consent, cannot make himself a slave to an outside being. *Eleutheria* is the perfection of this free will which prompts the will to do only good. It is the state where passions have no control to swerve the free will from doing good.[10] This reaches its perfection when man submits his free will completely to the service of God by remaining always fixed on virtuous doing, freed completely from the servitude of the devil's captivity (*aixmalosia*).[11]

ANTHROPOLOGY AFTER SIN

Because sin is a turning away from the ultimate good of man's nature, God, it could not be found in man's nature. It had to come from outside; it was *para physin*, outside nature, either running parallel to nature and never making contact with it or running diametrically opposed to it. When sin made contact with nature, the harmony in man's nature between the *autexousion*, free will, and *eleutheria*, the constancy in doing the good freely chosen, was destroyed. Distension was introduced as going against nature. That was a new element not found in the *opus Dei*, neither in creation nor in regeneration. The animal *passions* entered man's nature in the sense of St. Paul's *sarx*, the element in man rooted in his materiality that refuses to submit himself to God as to his supreme Other and binds him inextricably to multiplied creatures as nourishment for man's further *incentration* into himself as self-sufficient and independent of God. We must note here, almost never is nature conceived as a *natura lapsa*, a fallen nature. Evagrius says: "For from nature no evil thought enters because we were not in the beginning created evil, rather, 'the Lord sowed good seed in his field.' "[12] If there is evil in man, it could not come from his nature, the source of all good because it has come completely from God, but it must come from outside man's nature.

What did man lose through sin? He lost the similitude or likeness to God. He could never lose the image, *kat'eikona* but this image could be sullied.[13] Man acquired, if we can use this word, the necessity now of recuperating or recovering this likeness to God that was lost by sin. If one were to say to an early Greek Father: "Nothing is good except what is according to man's nature, *kata physin*," all passions, conceived now as the root of evil, would be excluded and condemned. Passions in rebellion are not natural or from nature, but come to nature from outside.

> God gave the commands to do good and to avoid sins, but opposing powers make us tend toward evil and it becomes difficult to do good. These sinful powers are not innate to nature (*symphytoi*) but are brought in from the outside (*epeisaktoi*). For this reason the Lord orders us to uproot and plant, dig up and rebuild.[14]

Macarius insists also that the passions have "come to" human nature from outside.

193

Therefore he who says that the cause of the ignominy of the passions is that they are from nature and not accidents, (*symbebikosi*) has changed the truth of God into a real lie. As I said above, the immaculate and pure God prepared man's image to His own, but by the jealousy of the devil, death entered into the world . . . From these words of Christ: 'Every planting not done by my Father will be uprooted' (Matt. 15, 13) and 'Because every creature of God is good' (I Tim. 4, 4), learn that the passions rooted in us are not ours but come from another source (*allotria*).[15]

Under the attack of the devil through the eight passions, man with God's help must now engage in the invisible battle, the spiritual warfare, in order to drive out of his nature all that did not come to it from the hand of God and to restore this nature to its pristine likeness to God. Thus we can understand why the psychology or rather pathology of the eight vices or passions and their "cure" occupies so predominant a place in the writings of the Fathers.[16] The spiritual life, viewed as an interior battle, is not merely a negative process of cutting out the evil presented by the devils to the noblest faculty of man, his intellect, but the positive virtues are supposed to be developed during the fray. This leads us to the divine model of reintegration, Christ.

ANTHROPOLOGY
AS RESTORED IN CHRIST

Irenaeus is the first theologian to formulate a restored anthropology in Christ. Man, fallen by sin, had lost the similitude to God. The Incarnation was necessary to regain it.

> The Word of God was made a son of man
> in order that man may receive the adop-
> tion and become a son of God . . . How
> could we have been able to be united to
> incorruptibility and immortality if Incor-
> ruptibility and Immortality did not first
> become that which we are?[17]

Christ shows forth to men the perfect Image of God; He restores the similitude or likeness of God to man.[18] Christ communicates the Spirit who perfects man.[19] In a theological synthesis amazing for its time, the double mysticism of St. John and St. Paul coalesce. Irenaeus mingles the two elements: the identification of the flesh of Christ with ours and the promise of eternal life because Christ is the Prince of Life who lives ontologically within us through grace.

Origen continues the doctrine of Irenaeus. The Incarnated Word takes upon Himself our nature (the image of man) and by means of His humanity He destroys in us the works of the devil by destroying the seed of the wicked and bringing forth in us the seed of God.[20] Athanasius, in fighting the Arian heresy, simplified Origen's restoration in order to find in the Christological theology a more solid defense for the faith.

> The Divine Word was made man that we
> might become gods. He was made visible
> through His body in order that we might
> have an idea of the invisible Father. He
> has supported the outrages of men in order
> that we may have a part of His immortal-
> ity.[21]

St. Gregory of Nyssa develops the reintegration of the image of God through the Divine Image made Man in a sacramental theology. Through Baptism man is purified from sin and united once again to God. Through the Eucharist Christ unites His divinized flesh to ours in order to divinize us. The other Cappadocians, St. Basil and St. Gregory of Nazianzus, also appeal to this sacramental diviniza-tion through Christ working in our souls by the transforming effects of grace; but St. Cyril of Alex-andria best synthesizes the doctrine of the preceding Fathers. If Christ did not become man He would not have transformed our humanity that had been deprived of its divine nobility. It is the property of the Holy Spirit to deify our human nature, first in Baptism when we become through the Holy Spirit temples of God, and the work of sanctifica-tion is begun anew. Holy Eucharist, the flesh of Christ deified through union with the Divine Word, becomes the instrument of divinization of our flesh.[22] Maximus the Confessor, whose doctrine space did not permit us to study in detail, unites the tradition of the East and the West in an admirable unity of theological expression that preserves the image-similitude of the Eastern Fathers and still injects the clarity of the Western distinction between nature and supernatural elevation through grace. For him, Christ and His Incarnation are the key to the ulti-mate explanation of creation. In Christ human nature was received into the subsistence of a Divine Person. So likewise, it became conceiveable and pos-sible that that same human nature in men could be called (elevated) to a divine condition without lessening or changing its integral makeup. To ac-complish this divinization in man's nature,

> . . . it was necessary that He who is truly
> the author of creatures according to their
> nature should become also through grace
> the artisan of the divinization of those
> creatures in order that He who gave being
> should appear also as giving abundance of
> eternal well-being. Such is the work of
> the Word Incarnate. He has renewed the
> dispositions of nature and through His own
> Incarnation gave the gift of supernatural

grace, divinization, to human nature.[23]

In a very summary fashion we have tried to present the main lines of the patristic theological anthropology of man's nature, built around the image-likeness concept of Genesis. Fr. Crouzel says that the patristic teaching of image offers an integrated synthesis of all theology in explaining how man comes from God and how he must return to God through his perfect model, Christ, the Image of the Father.[24] The fact that this concept developed within the history of concrete salvation, beginning with God's initial creation, man's free rejection of this divinization through sin, the restoration of this primitive filiation with God through the Divine Son made man, the ever progressing movement of sanctification through the Holy Spirit working in the human soul to refashion it in the imitation of Christ, gives us an ontological dynamism that is verified in Scripture and in the spiritual life of each individual.

But one must not be content with this synthesis. It has its lacunae and deficiencies. Through the use of metaphors such as image, likeness, model, mirror, sun and light rays, this whole doctrine, designed to explain the relation of God with finite man, the inter-relation of nature and grace, can be relegated to a lack of precision in speech and concept that leaves us with mere verbalism. The theology of the Eastern Fathers is bound intimately with their doctrine of the spiritual life. Theology is the science about God and the spiritual life in the concrete striving towards God as man's ultimate goal. Perhaps from a deeper study of patristic theology, especially anthropology as seen by the Greek Fathers in the intimate relationship to the spiritual life, Western theology can regain something of its existential dynamism and theology will become again a *life in God*. The Eastern theology can profit by being complemented in this doctrine of image by the teaching of St. Augustine and St. Thomas.[25] They both have used the image and similitude in working out a theological anthropology. Through much debating under the attacks of various heresies against grace, they were able to fashion concepts capable of clearly distinguishing the various points of relationship between nature in its different historical and possible stages, and grace.

The Eastern tradition, with its fresh insight into the central truth of the Christian message that God condescends in His activities, especially through the God-Man, Jesus Christ, to make us into new creatures, "participators in the divine nature" (II Pet. 1, 4), can keep before the Western mind, so gifted in logical thinking, this unique, ontological relationship between God and man. Man's whole nature is to become, through God's *energies* of grace working on him, a living image of his Creator.

The words of St. Gregory of Nyssa form a fitting close to this work, as they speak the reverent mind of all the early Eastern Fathers as they contemplate what it means that God should so love man as to create him according to His image and likeness.

> Man who among beings counts for nothing, who is dust, grass, vanity, who was adopted to be a son of the God of the universe, becomes the friend of this Being of such excellence and grandeur; this is a mystery that we can neither see nor understand nor comprehend. What thanks should man give for so great a favor? What word, what thought, what lifting up of mind in order to exalt the superabundance of this grace? Man surpasses his own very nature. From a mortal being he becomes immortal, from a perishable being he becomes imperishable. From ephemeral he becomes

eternal. In a word, from man he becomes god. In fact, rendered worthy to become a son of God, he will have in himself the dignity of the Father, enriched by all the inheritance of the goods of the Father. O munificence of the Lord, so bountiful . . . How great are the gifts of such ineffable treasures![26]

FOOTNOTES TO INTRODUCTION

1. Camelot, P.Th., O.P., "La Theologie de l'Image de Dieu" in *Revue des Sciences Phil. et Théol.*, 1956, pgs. 443-471.
2. Genesis 1:26. The monk Meletius in his treatise on man (PG 64,1076 C) says that the Fathers did not follow the example of the pagan philosophers in their approach to human nature, but rather dealt with it only in relation to God and human salvation.
3. Bulgakov, S., "De Verbe Incarne" in *La Sagesse Divine et la Théanthropie*, Paris, 1943, pgs. 65-68.
4. Col. 1:15.
5. Brunner, Emil, *Man in Revolt*, London, 1953, pgs. 97-98.
6. Rahner, Karl, "Person" in *Theological Dictionary*, New York, 1965, pg. 351.
7. Col. 3:10.
8. *Adv. Haereses* III, 19; PG 7,939 B.

FOOTNOTES TO CHAPTER ONE

1. 1 John 4:9-10.
2. 1 John 4:16.
3. Genesis 1:26.
4. 2 Cor. 5:17-19.
5. *Super-Humanity, Super-Christ, Super-Charity* (private translation).
6. Cf: Evagrius, *De Oratione*, Ch. 50 in Hausherr, I., *Les Lecons d'un Contemplatif. Le Traité de l'Oraison d'Evagre le Pontique*, pgs. 72-75, Paris, 1960. Also, Maximus the Confessor, *Ad Thalassium*, PG 90, 372 B-C.
7. John 3:16.
8. John 10:10.
9. *In Joannem* II, PG 14, 16, 152; 10, 141-144.
10. Hebr. 13:8.
11. *Theatetes*, 176 B.
12. *Timaeus*, 92 C; *Parmenides*, 132 C.
13. 1 John 3:2.
14. Gal. 3:26.
15. *In Joan.* II, PG 14, 2, 108-109.
16. Ps. 81: 6.
17. Jn. 14:6.
18. Col. 1:14-18.
19. *Homilia in Genesim*, I, 13, PG 12, 93-96.
20. *Homilia in Genesim*, I, 15, PG 12, 101.
21. Matt. 5:48.
22. De Lubac, H., S.J., *Surnaturel; Etudes Historiques*, pgs. 477-480; 483-494, Paris, 1946. Cf: the review of this book by Malevez, L., S.J., in *Nouvelle Revue Théologique*, T. 69, Jan., 1947, pgs. 3-31.
23. Cf: Rudberg, G., "Hellenisches Schauen," in *Classica et Mediaevalia*, pgs. 159-186, no. 5, 1942; Hausherr, I., S.J., "Les grands courants de la spiritualité oriental" in *Orientalia*

Christiana Periodica, 1, Pgs. 114-138, Rome, 1935; Le
Maitre, "Contemplation chez les Peres orientaux," in *Dict.
de Spiritualité*, Vol. 2; van der Aalst, P., A. A., "Contemplation et Hellenisme," in *Proche-Orient Chrétien*, T.
14, Fasc. 2, July-Sept., 1964, pgs. 151-168.

24. Cf: Ps. 21: 5; 91:16; 34:12.
25. Deut. 4:1.
26. 1 Sam. 2:6; Amos 9:2; Hos. 13:14.
27. Dan. 12:2.
28. John 20:31.
29. Pastor Hermes, *Simil*. 9:16.
30. Ignatius, *Epistle to the Ephesians*, 11:1; *Magnesians*, 12;
    Ephesians, 9:2; 15:3.
31. Prov. 3:18.
32. Jaeger, Werner, *Early Christianity and Greek Paideia*,
    Cambridge, 1961.
33. Hausherr, I., S.J., *Les Lecons . . . op. cit.*, pgs. 76-78.
34. De Lubac, H., S.J., *op.cit.*, pg. 493.
35. Book III, Ch. 54;55.
36. *Vitae Patrum*, Lib. VI, PL 73, 1019 D.
37. Mersch, E., S.J., *The Whole Christ*, Milwaukee, Wis.,
    1938, pg. 295.
38. Danielou J., S.J., *Platonisme et Théologie Mystique;
    Doctrine Spirituelle de St. Grégoire de Nysse*, Aubier,
    1944, pg. 50.
39. *Adversus Haereses IV*, 64 (Abbrev.: Adv. Haer.).
40. *Adv. Haer.* III, 19, 1 & 3, PG 7, 938-941.
41. Col. 1:15.

FOOTNOTES TO CHAPTER TWO

1. John 17:3.
2. 2 Pet. 1:4.
3. Gilson, E., *The Mystical Theology of St. Bernard*, N.Y.,
   1940, pg. 120.
4. Jn. 14:23-24.
5. Cf: Lebreton, J., S.J., *History of the Dogma of the Trinity
   from its Origin to the Council of Nicaea*, Vol. 1, N.Y.,
   1939, pg. 46.
6. Wood, C. T., *The Life, Letters and Religion of St. Paul*,
   Edinburgh, 1925, pg. 320.
7. Zeller, Ed., *Die Philosophie der Griechen in ihrer geschichtlichen Entwicklung*, Vol. 4, no. 1, Hildesheim, 1963, pg. 67.
8. Cf: Bréhier, E., *Les idées philosophiques et religieuses de
   Philon d'Alexandrie*, Paris, 1908.
9. Prov. 8:22.
10. Jn. 1:2-4, 14.
11. Jaeger, Werner, *op. cit.* Cf: Danielou, Jean, *Histoire des
    doctrines chrétiennes avant Nicée II: Message evangelique
    et culture hellenistique*, Paris, 1961.
12. Justin, *First Apology*, Ch. 46, pg. 178. Citations from:
    The Ante-Nicene Fathers, editors: Roberts, A. and Donald-

son, J., Grand Rapids, Mich., Vol. 1, *The Apostolic Fathers, Justin Martyr, Irenaeus.*

13. Justin, *Second Apology,* Ch. 10, pgs. 191-192.
14. Danielou, Jean, *Les Saints Paiens de l'Ancien Testament,* Paris, 1956, pgs. 28-29.
15. Lagrange, Marie-Joseph, *Saint Justin,* Paris, 1910, pg. 163.
16. *Dialogue with Trypho,* Ch. 62, pg. 228.
17. *Ibid.,* Ch. 56, pgs. 223-224.
18. *First Apology,* Ch. 22, pg. 170.
19. *Dialogue with Trypho,* Ch. 61, pg. 227.
20. Quasten, J., *Patrology,* Vol. 1, Westminster, Md., 1950, pg. 209.
21. Lagrange, M. J., *op. cit.,* pgs. 172-173.
22. *Dialogue with Trypho,* Ch. 62, pg. 228: "This offspring . . . . from the Father was with the Father before all creatures."
23. Matt. 3:27.
24. Jn. 1:18.

FOOTNOTES TO CHAPTER THREE

1. Eusebius, *Historia Ecclesiastica,* Book 5,20,5-7 in *A Select Library of Nicene and Post-Nicene Fathers of the Christian Church,* 2nd Series, ed. Schaff, P. and Wace, H., Vol. 1, *Eusebius of Caesarea: Church History* (abbrev. LNPF), pgs. 238-239.
2. Irenaeus, *Adv. Haer.* I, Ch. 5,5, ANF (Citations from: *The Ante-Nicene Fathers;* Vol. 1; ed. Roberts, A. and Donaldson, J., Grand Rapids, Mich.) pg. 323.
3. *Adv. Haer.* I, Ch. 6, pg. 324.
4. *Ibid.,* pg. 326.
5. Gross, Jules, *La divinisation du chrétien d'aprés les péres grecs,* Paris, 1938, pg. 132.
6. *Adv. Haer.* IV, Ch. 38, pgs. 521-522.
7. For other places where he links image and likeness together as synonomous cf. *Adv. Haer.* III, Ch. 18, 1, pg. 446; Ch. 22,1, pg. 454; Ch. 23-1-2, pgs. 455-456; IV, Ch. 38,3-4, pgs. 521-522; V, Ch. 1,3, pg. 527; V, Ch. 12,4, pgs. 538-539; IV, Ch. 20,1, pgs. 487-488; IV, preface, 4, pgs. 462-463.
8. *Proof of the Apostolic Preaching* (hereafter listed as *Demonst.*) tr. by Smith, J. P., S. J., in *Ancient Christian Writers,* Westminster, Md., 1952, Vol. 16, Ch. 22, pg. 61. Cf: Ch. 11, pg. 54; Ch. 55, pg. 83.
9. *Adv. Haer.* V, Ch. 9,1, pg. 534. Cf: V, Ch. 6,1, pgs. 531-532.
10. *Ibid,* V, Ch. 6,1, pgs. 531-532. *Demonst.,* Ch. 2, pg. 48.
11. *Adv. Haer.* V, Ch. 6,1; pgs. 531-532.
12. Cf: *Adv. Haer.* V, Ch. 9,1-3, pgs. 534-535; Ch. 8,1, pg. 533; Ch. 10, 1 pg. 536; Ch. 12,2, pgs. 537-538; IV, Ch. 20,4 and 6, pgs. 488-489. *Demonst.,* Ch. 7, pgs. 151-152.
13. *Adv. Haer.* IV, Ch. 11,2, pg. 474.

14. *Ibid.,* IV, Ch. 38, 3, pg. 521.
15. *Ibid.,* IV, Ch. 39,2-3, pgs. 522-523.
16. *Ibid.,* IV, Ch. 6,2, pg. 468.
17. Eph. 1:10. Cf: Schlier, H., "Anakephaloiomai" in *Theo-logisches Worterbuch,* III, pg. 681 ss. Also Cerfaux, L., *Christ in the Theology of St. Paul,* 2nd ed., N. Y., 1959, pg. 424.
18. *Adv. Haer.* I, Ch. 10,1, pg. 330.
19. *Adv. Haer.* III, Ch. 18,7, pg. 448.
20. Mersch, Emil, *The Whole Christ,* Milwaukee, 1938, pg. 230. The word *anakephaloiosis* has a more intricate history and meaning than that which Mersch presents. According to J. Lawson, *The Biblical Theology of St. Irenaeus,* London, 1948, pg. 140 ss., Gustav Molwitz, in his Latin work *De 'anakephaloioseos' in Irenaei Potestate,* Dresden, 1874, is the first scholar to treat of its meaning. He points out that the word does not come from *kephale,* meaning head; hence, (contrary to many translators of St. Paul, Eph. 1:10) does not refer to the summing up of things under a head (Christ), but the word comes from *kephalaion,* meaning the chief point or summary, the whole containing the parts. Lawson gathers together all possible interpreta-tions of Irenaeus' complicated term and offers as the chief interpretation the meanings: to unite under a single head, to restore to the original, to make a new start, to bring to a climax, to go over the ground a second time.
21. Cf: Aulen, Gustav, *Christus Victor,* London, 1931.
22. Cf: *Adv. Haer.* V, Ch. 21,1, pg. 549; V, Ch. 16,3 pg. 544; V, Ch. 17,3-4, pgs. 545-546; V, Ch. 19,1, pg. 547; V, Ch. 23,2, pgs. 551-552; *Demonst.,* Ch. 34, pgs. 69-70.
23. *Adv. Haer.* III, Ch. 19,1, pgs. 448-449; also: III, Ch. 10,2, pg. 424; IV, Ch. 33,4, pg. 507; IV, Ch. 38.4, pg. 522; IV, Ch. 39,2, pg. 523.
24. *Adv. Haer.* IV, Ch. 34, pg. 511.
25. *Ibid,* V, Ch. 9,2, pg. 535; also, 3-4, pg. 535.
26. *Ibid.,* II, Ch. 34,3, pg. 411.
27. Congar, M-I., O.P., "La deification dans la tradition spirituelle de l' Orient" in *La Vie Spirituelle,* T.43, 1935, pgs. 99-100.
28. *Adv. Haer.* V, Ch. 10,1-2, pg. 536.
29. *Ibid.,* V, Ch. 12,2, pg. 537.
30. *Ibid.,* V, Ch. 13, pg. 539; V, Ch. 10-Ch. 17, pgs. 536-546 contain many texts to illustrate this point.
31. *Demonst.,* Ch. 5, pg. 51. See also *Demonstr.,* Ch. 97, pg. 108.
32. *Ibid.,* Ch. 6, pg. 51.
33. *Ibid.*
34. Some writers, as M. J. Turmel, *Histoire des dogmes,* T.4, Paris, 1935, pgs. 451-465, apparently err in saying the early Fathers did not make the distinction between uncreated and created grace.
35. Cf: Gross, Jules, *op. cit.,* pgs. 156-157.

36. *Adv. Haer.* V, Ch. 6,1, pgs. 531-532; V, Ch. 12,2 pgs. 537-538; III, Ch. 6,1, pgs. 418-419.
37. *Ibid.*, IV, Ch. 39,1, pg. 522.
38. *Ibid.*, V, Ch. 28,4, pg. 557. The latter quote is from the Epistle of St. Ignatius of Antioch to the Romans, Ch. 4.
39. *Ibid.*, V, 36,1, pg. 566.
40. *Ibid.*, pgs. 566-567.
41. *Ibid.*, Ch. 36,3, pg. 567.

FOOTNOTES TO CHAPTER FOUR

1. *Paedagogos* (hereafter abbrev. as *Paed.*), II, Ch. 1, pg. 241. All citations are from the works of Clement as found in *The Ante-Nicene Fathers*, op. cit., Vol. 2.
2. *Stromata* (hereafter abbrev. *Strom.*), I, Ch. 28, pgs. 340-341.
3. Quasten, J., *Patrology*, Vol. 2, Westminster, Md., 1953, pg. 12.
4. *Strom.* VI, Ch. 12, pg. 502.
5. Probably a quote from a hymn.
6. *Protrepticos* (hereafter abbrev. as *Protrep.*), Ch. 1, pg. 172.
7. *Ibid.*
8. *Protrep.*, Ch. 10, pg. 199.
9. *Ibid.*, pg. 200.
10. *Strom.* II, Ch. 19, pg. 370. Cf: *Strom.* VI, Ch. 16, pgs. 512.
11. *Ibid.*, V, Ch. 14, pg. 466.
12. *Strom.* II, Ch. 22, pg. 376. Cf: *Paed.* I, Ch. 12, pg. 234.
13. *Strom.* VI, Ch. 12, pg. 502.
14. *Ibid.*, II, Ch. 19, pg. 369.
15. *Ibid.*, VI, Ch. 16, pg. 511. Cf: *Paed.* III, Ch. 12, pg. 291.
16. *Protrep.*, Ch. 1, pg. 174.
17. *Theatetes*, 176 B.
18. Cf: Hausherr, I., S.J., *Les Lecons. . . . op. cit.*
19. John Climacus thus describes the "impassible man": "The man, who really loves the Lord, who has made a real effort to find the coming Kingdom, who has really begun to be troubled by his sins, who is really mindful of eternal torment and judgement, who really lives in fear of his own departure, will not love, care or worry about money, or possessions, or parents, or worldly glory, or friends, or brothers, or anything at all on earth. But, having shaken off all ties with earthly things and having stripped himself of all his cares and having come to have even his own flesh and having stripped himself of everything, he will follow Christ without anxiety or hesitation, always looking heavenward and expecting help from there. . ." (*Scalae*, Gradus 2, PG 88, 653 C).
20. *Strom.* VI, Ch. 9, pgs. 496-497.
21. *Ibid.*, pg. 497.
22. *Ibid.*
23. *Ibid.*

24. Cf: Faller, Otto, S.J., "Griechische Vergottung und Christliche Vergottlichung" in *Gregorianum*, VI, (1925) pg. 405 ss.
25. Gross, J., *op. cit.*, pg. 163.
26. *Strom.* V, Ch. 1, pg. 444.
27. *Strom.* VI, Ch. 1, pg. 523; *Strom.* IV, Ch. 21, pg. 433; *Paed.* I, Ch. 6, pg. 216.
28. Lebreton, J., "Le desaccord de la foi populaire et de la théologie savante dans l'Eglise du III siécle" in *Revue d'histoire ecclesiastique,* T.19, 1923, pg. 493.
29. *Strom.* V, Ch. 1, pg. 444.
30. *Ibid.*
31. *Strom.* II, Ch. 19, pg. 369.
32. *Ibid., IV,* Ch. 22, pg. 434.
33. *Ibid.,* V, Ch. 9, pgs. 496-497.
34. *Ibid.,* pg. 497.
35. *Ibid.*
36. *Strom.* VI, Ch. 12, pg. 503.
37. *Ibid.,* pg. 504.
38. Tollington, R. B., *Clement of Alexandria—A Study in Christian Liberalism,* Vol. 2, London, 1914, pgs. 99-100.

FOOTNOTES TO CHAPTER FIVE

The following works form the sources of the citations from Origen's writings.
1. Migne: *Patrologiae cursus completus, series graeca.* Abbrev. PG.
    : *Patrologiae cursus completus, series Latina.* Abbrev. PL.
2. *Die griechischen christlichen Schriftsteller der ersten drei Jahrhunderte,* Berlin edition. Abbrev. GCS.
3. *The Ante-Nicene Fathers, op. cit.* Abbrev. ANF
4. *Ancient Christian Writers,* Westminster, Md. Abbrev. ACW.
5. Scheier, J., *Entrétien d'Origene avec Heraclide et les eveques, ses colleques, sur le Pére, le fils et l'ame,* Cairo, 1949. Abbrev. *Entr. Her.*
1. The outstanding work on Origen's doctrine of the image and likeness is the recently published work of Crouzel, Henri, S. J., *Théologie de l'Image de Dieu chez Origene,* Aubier, 1955. Most helpful also is his most recent work, *Origene et la "Connaissance Mystique,"* Desclée de Brouwer, 1961.
    Other works on Origen that can be consulted with profit are:
    Bardy, G., *Origene, Collection Les Moralistes Chrétiens,* Paris, 1931.
    Bardy, G., "Origene" in *Dictionnaire Théologique Catholique,* T.11, 1489-1565.
    Prat, F., *Origene,* Paris, 1907.
    Prat, F., "Origene" in *Dictionnaire de la Bible,* Letouzey et Ane, 1908, T.4, 1870.

Cadiou, R., *Introduction au system d'Origene*, Paris, 1932.

Cadiou, R., *La Jeunesse d'Origene*, Paris, 1953.

Bertrand, F., *Mystique de Jesus chez Origene*, Collection *Théologie*, Aubier, Paris, 1951.

Danielou, J., *Origen*, New York, 1955.

Denis, J., *De la philosophie d'Origene*, Paris, 1884.

De Faye, E., *Origene, Bibliotheque de l'Ecole des Hautes Etudes*, 3 vols., Paris, 1923-1928.

De Faye, E., *Esquisse de la pensée d'Origene, Bibliotheque historique des religions*, Paris, 1925.

Freppel, Msgr. Ch. E., *Origene. Cours d'eloquence sacrée*, 2 vols, Paris, 1888.

Kyrillos, Msgr. II, *Reconstitution de la synthese scientifique d'Origene*, 2 vols., Alexandria, 1907.

Volker, W., *Das Volkommenheitsideal des Origenes. Beitrage zur historischen Theologie*, Tubingen, 1931.

2. Col. 1:15; 2 Cor. 4:4.
3. Jn. 1:**18**.
4. Matt. 11:27.
5. *De Principiis* I, Ch. 1,8, ANF, pg. 245.
6. *De Princ.* I, Ch. 2,4, pg. 247.
7. *Ibid.*, 9, pg. 249.
8. *Ibid.*, 4, pg. 247.
9. *In Hebr.*, Fragm. 24, 359, PG 14, 1303 C-D; PG 17,580 C-581.
10. Origen's double creation interpretation is found in many passages. Cf: *In Rom.* II, 13, PG 14,913 A; *In Joan. XX*, 19, PG 14,617; *In Cant.*, Prol. PG 13,65 A; *In Matt.* XIV, 16, GCS, 10, pg. 321. 1.23 ss.
11. Gen. 1:26-27.
12. Gen. 2:7.
13. *De Princ.* II, Ch. 9, 3-4, ANF, pg. 290-291.
14. *In Rom.*, I, 19, PG 14,871 A. Also *Entr. Her.* II, pg. 146, 1.10 ss.
15. *In Joan.* XX, 19, PG 14,617. For the distinction between *poiein* and *plattein* see: *Sel. in Ps.* 99, 2, PG 12,168 B-C; *In Cant.* Prol., PG 13, 65 A.
16. *Hom. in Gen.* 1,13, PG 12,93-96.
17. For his distinction between *nous*, created in a preexistence before the body, and *psyche* or animal soul, created with the body, see: *Fragm. In Luc.* 53, GCS 9, pg. 259, 1.40 ss.
18. *De Princ.* II, Ch. 8,1, ANF, pg. 286. *Contra Cels.* IV, 85, ANF, pg. 535.
19. *De Princ.* I, Ch. 7,4, pg. 263.
20. Slomkowski, A., *L'état primitif de l'homme dans la tradition de l'église avant saint Augustin*, Paris, 1928, pg. 54.
21. *In Levit.* XIII, 3, PG 12,496 A.
22. *In Rom.* X, 14, PG 14,1275 A.
23. *In Joan.* XIII, 37, PG 14,464 A-B.
24. *Hom. in Gen.* I, 13, PG 12,93-96.
25. *De Princ.* III, Ch. 6,1, pg. 344. *Contra Cels.* IV, 30, pgs. 509-510.
26. *In Joan.* XX, 20, PG 14,621 B.

27. *De Princ.* II, Ch. 3,4 pg. 275. *Hom. in Gen.* I, 13, PG 12,93-96.

28. *In Joan.* XX, 22, PG 14,625. *Contra Cels.* IV, 30, pgs. 509-510.

29. *De Princ.* III, Ch. 6,1, pg. 344.

30. *Contra Cels.* IV, 3,11, pg. 498; 501. *De Princ.* 1, Ch. 2,7, pg. 248.

31. *De Princ.* I, Ch. 6, pg. 260.

32. Cadiou, R., *Introduction au system d'Origene,* Paris, 1932.

33. Danielou, J., S.J., *Origen,* N.Y. 1955, pgs. 287-288.

34. *De Princ.* IV, Ch. 1, 11, pg. 359. *Contra Cels.* VI, Ch. 13, pg. 579. *Hom in Rom.* VI, 14, PG 14,1102.

35. Danielou, *op. cit.,* pg. 276.

36. *In Joan.* XIX, 6, PG 14,569 B.

37. *Hom. In Gen.* XIII, 3, PG 12,232 C.

38. *In Joan.* I, 30, PG 14,77 A; *ibid.,* II, 3,113.

39. *In Joan.* XIX, 1 PG 14,536.

40. *Ibid.,* XXXII, 18,820 C.

41. *Ibid.,* I, 33,77-80. *De Princ.* II, Ch. 11,3, ANF, pg. 297.

42. *De Princ.* I, Ch. 8,4, pg. 266.

43. *Hom. in Cant.* I, 10, PG 13,472 B. *Hom. in Exod.* VII, 6, PG 12,347 A-B.

44. *De Princ.* I, Ch. 3,7, pg. 254.

45. *Ibid.,* I, Ch. 3,8, pg. 255.

46. *Comm. in Cant.* III, 10, PG 13,181 A-C.

47. *De Oratione,* Ch. 2,4, pgs. 19-21 in ACW (tr. J. J. O'Meara, Westminster, Md., 1954).

48. PL 23,7,360; *ibid.,* 25,375 B; PL 22,747; 749; 1063; 1067; 763; 783.

49. Bardy, G., *"Origene"* in DTC, 11,1545 ss.
   Cadiou, R., *La Jeunesse . . . op. cit.,* pg. 120 ss.
   Prat, F., *Origene,* Paris, 1907, pgs. 41,88.
   Bigg, Ch., *The Christian Platonists of Alexandria,* Oxford, 1886, pg. 225.

50. *De Princ.* Praef. 5, ANF, pg. 240.

51. Crouzel, H., *Théol. de l'Image . . . op. cit.,* pg. 249 ss.

52. *Sel. in Ps.* 1, 51, PG 12,1093 B

53. Jenkins, C., "Fragm. in I Cor. LXXXIV on I Cor. XV: 20-30" in *Journal of Theological Studies,* Oxford, 1908-1909, T.10, pg. 46 ss., cited by H. Crouzel, *op. cit.,* pg. 249, footnote no. 11. Cf: *Entr. Her., op. cit.,* pg. 132, 1.4 ss.

54. *In Matt.* XV, 23, GCS, 10, pg. 417, 1.17 ss.

55. Cf: Edsman, C. E., *Le Flueve de feu,* cited by J. Danielou, *op. cit.,* pg. 61.

56. *De Princ.* II, Ch. 11,7, ANF, pg. 300.

57. *De Princ.* Praef. 5, pg. 240.

58. *In Matt.* XIII, 21, GCS 10, pg. 239, 1.4 ss, pg. 254, 1.21, cited by H. Crouzel, *op. cit.,* pg. 252.

59. *In Joan.* I, 16, PG 14,49 D.

60. 2 Peter 1:3-4.

FOOTNOTES TO CHAPTER SIX

1. Cf: Le Bachelet, X., "Athanase" in DTC Vol. 12, 2166.
2. Some references to recent works on Athanasius: Bardy, G., *Saint Athanase*, Paris, 1925; Berchem, J. B., *Le Role du Verbe dans l'Oeuvre de la Creation et de la Sanctification d'aprés Saint Athanase*, Angelicum, Rome, 1938; Bouyer, L., *L'Incarnation et l'Eglise-Corps du Christ dans la Théologie de Saint Athanase*, Paris, 1943; Gaudel, A., "La Théologie du Logos chez Saint Athanase" in *Revue des Sciences religeuses*, Strasbourg, 1929, 1931; Bernard, Régis, *L'Image de Dieu d'aprés Saint Athanase*, Paris, 1952; Le Bachelet, X., "Athanase" in DTC, Vol. 12, 2166 ss.
3. Pollard, T. E., "Logos and Son in Origen, Arius and Athansius" in *Studia Patristica*, Berlin, 1957, Vol. 2, pg. 287.
4. *First Discourse against the Arians*, 9, LNPF, pg. 311. All citations of St. Athanasius, unless otherwise indicated, are from: *A Select Library of Nicene and Post-Nicene Fathers of the Christian Church*, 2nd Series; ed. Philip Schaff and Henry Wace, Vol. 4, *St. Athanasius. Select Works and Letters*, Grand Rapids, Mich., 1957, abbrev. LNPF. Cf: *Second Discourse*, 38, pg. 368.
5. *Discourse III*, 5, pg. 396.
6. *De Decretis*, 27, pg. 168.
7. *Contra Gentes*, 46, pg. 29.
8. *Op. cit.*, pg. 27.
9. *De Incarnatione*, 13, pg. 43.
10. *De Incarn*, 11, pg. 42.
11. *Contra Gentes*, 8, pg. 8.
12. *De Incarn.*, 3, pg. 37.
13. *Ibid.*, 4, pg. 38.
14. *Contra Gentes*, 8, pg. 8.
15. *De Incarn.*, 14, pg. 43.
16. *Ibid.*, 4, pg. 38.
17. *Ibid.*, 6, pg. 39.
18. *Ibid.*, 6, pg. 39.
19. *Ibid.*, 13, pg. 43.
20. *Ibid.*, 14, pg. 43. Cf: the analysis of this word and its cognates by R. Bernard, *op. cit.*, pgs. 53-54.
21. *De Incarn.*, 15,16, pgs. 44-45.
22. *Ibid.*, 9, pgs. 40-41.
23. *Adv. Haer.* IV, 38,4;V, 9,2.
24. *De Incarn.*, 54, pg. 65.
25. *Ad Adelphinum, Epist.* 60,4, pg. 576.
26. *Ad Maximum, Epist.* 61, 2, pgs. 578-579.
27. *De Synodis*, 51, pg. 477.
28. *Contra Arianos* II, 70 pg. 386.
29. Strater, H., *Die Erlosungslehre des hl. Athanasius*, Fribourg-en-Brisgau, 1894, pg. 140.
30. *Contra Arianos* III, 33, pgs. 411-412.
31. *De Incarn. et Contra Arianos*, 5, PG 26,992.
32. Gross J., *op. cit.*, pg. 210.

33. *Ad Serapionem* I, 20, PG 26, 577 C. Also, *ibid.,* 24,585-588; 30,597-600.
34. *Ibid.,* 31,601 A.
35. *Ibid.,* 23,585 A-B.
36. *Ibid.,* 31,605 A.
37. *Ibid.,* 25,589 B.
38. Bernard, R., *op. cit.,* pgs. 127-130.
39. *Ad Serap.* I, 20, PG 26,577 B.
40. *Ibid.,* 24, 588 B.
41. *Ibid.,* 26, 592 B.
42. *Ad Serap.* IV, 3, 640 D-641 A.
43. Bernard, *op. cit.,* pg. 128.
44. *Ad Serap.* IV, 21,672 C, cited by Bernard, *op. cit.,* pg. 130.
45. *Ad Serap.* I, 20,577 C.
46. *Vita S. Antonii,* 7, pg. 197; 14, pg. 200; 19, pg. 201; 55, pg. 211.
47. *Ibid.,* 5, pg. 197.
48. *Ibid.,* 20, pg. 201.
49. *Ibid.*

FOOTNOTES TO CHAPTER SEVEN

1. *Haexameron,* cited from: *A Select Library of Nicene and Post-Nicene Fathers of the Christian Church,* 2nd series, Vol. 8, Grand Rapids, Mich., 1955, abbrev. as LNPF, *Homily* IX, 6, pg. 107.
2. *Ibid.,* pgs. 106-107.
3. *Homily on Ps.* 48, cited from *The Fathers of the Church,* Catholic University of America, Wash., D.C., 1963, Vol. 46, pgs. 324-325. In a similar way we find in the Byzantine Liturgy of St. Basil, which text was surely not composed originally by Basil but at least was edited and approved by him, in the Trisagion prayer: " . . . (You, God) who brought all things into being out of nothingness and created man according to Your image and likeness and adorned him with all the gifts of Your grace. . ." In the Anaphora we read: ". . . Our Lord Jesus Christ, great God and Redeemer, our hope, who is the image of Your goodness, the seal of Your own likeness. . ." and "for when You had formed man by taking dust from the earth and, stamping Your own image on him, O God, had placed him in a paradise of delights. . . ."
4. *Epistola* 233, LNPF, pg. 273.
5. *De Spiritu Sancto,* Ch. 1, 2, LNPF, pg. 2.
6. *Homilia in illud Attende,* 6, PG 31, 212 B.
7. *Ibid.*
8. Cf: Gaith, J., *La Conception de la liberté chez Grégoire de Nysse,* Paris, 1953.
9. *De Spiritu Sancto,* Ch. 1, 2, LNPF, pg. 2.
10. *Quod Deus non est auctor mali,* 6, PG 36, 344 B-C.
11. *Ibid.,* 345 B.
12. *Ibid.*

13. *Epistola* 233, LNPF, pg. 273.
14. *Ibid.*
15. *Quod Deus non est* . . . . PG 31, 344 B.
16. *Ibid.*
17. Cf: *De Princ.* of Origen, I, 3,8, PG 11,155 ss.
18. *Quod Deus non est.* . . . . PG 31,344 C.
19. Cf: Crouzel, H., *Théologie de l'Image* . . . *op. cit.,* pg. 206 ss.
20. *Homily 19 on Ps. 48, Frs. of the Ch.* Vol. 46, pg. 325.
21. *Ibid.,* pg. 316.
22. *Ibid.,* pg. 318.
23. *On the Judgement of God, Frs. of the Ch.,* Vol. 9, pg. 54.
24. *De Sp. Sancto,* Ch. 26, LNPF, Vol. 8, pg. 38.
25. *Ibid.*
26. Athanasius is much more explicit, proving the divinity of the Holy Spirit from the divinizing activities of the Holy Spirit in man. Basil was severely criticized by his contemporaries for not having called the Holy Spirit by the title of God and Athanasius even came to his defence. Cf: Quasten, J., *Patrology, op. cit.,* Vol. 3, pg. 231.
27. *De Sp. Sancto,* Ch. 9, 22, pg. 15.
28. *Epistola* 159, Vol. 8, LNPF, pg. 212.
29. *De Sp. Sancto,* Ch. 18, 47, pg. 29.
30. *Ibid.*
31. Ch. 26, 64, LNPF, pg. 40. It is interesting to note how often St. Athanasius, especially in his four letters to Serapion, speaks of the Holy Spirit in similar terms. Cf: *Ad Serap.* I, 24, PG 26,585 C-588 A; *ibid.,* 31,601 A; 20,577 C; 30,597-600; 23,585 A-B.
32. Cf: Amand, D., *L'ascese monastique de Saint Basile,* Maredsoud, 1948; Spidlik, T., S.J., *La Sophiologie de S. Basile,* Rome, 1961; Giet, S., *Les idées et l'action sociales de Saint Basile de Césarée,* Paris, 1932; Kranich, A., *Die Asketik in ihrer dogmatischen Gundlage bei Basilius dem Grossen,* Paderborn, 1896; Nothomb, D. M., Charité et Unité. Doctrine de Saint Basile le Grand sur la charité envers le prochain" in *Proche-Orient Chrétien,* 4, 1954, pgs. 309-321. 5, 1955, pgs. 3-13.
33. Von Campenhausen, Hans, *The Fathers of the Greek Church,* N.Y., 1959, pg. 95.
34. Gross, Jules, *op. cit.,* pg. 244.
35. *Stromata II,* 22, PG 8,1088.
36. PG 11,333; 412; 12,436.
37. *Oratio* 8, 6, LNPF, pg. 240. For other examples of this, cf: *Oratio* 33, 12 pg. 332; *Oratio* 37, 12, pg. 341.
38. *Oratio* 33, 12, LNPF, pg. 332.
39. *Oratio* 38, 11, LNPF, pg. 348.
40. *Poemata Dogmatica,* 9, 10,33, PG 37, 467.
41. *Poemata Moralia,* 10, 111-114, PG 37,688.
42. *Poemata Dogmatica,* 9, 1-3, PG 37, 446-447.
43. Pinault, Henri, *Platonisme de Saint Grégoire de Naizanze,* La Roche-Sur-Yon, 1925, pgs. 153-155.
44. *Oratio* 28, 17, LNPF, pg. 294.

45. *Oratio* 38, 12, LNPF, pg. 348. Cf: *Oratio* 45, 2nd Oration on Easter, 8, LNPF, pg. 425.
46. *Ibid.*, 13, pg. 349. We see almost identically this same passage repeated in *Oratio* 45, 9, LNPF, pgs. 425-426.
47. *Epistola ad Cledonium*, PG 38,181.
48. *Oratio*, 1, 4,5, LNPF, pg. 203.
49. *Oratio* 7 (Panegyric to his brother, Caesarius) 23, LNPF, pg. 237.
50. *Oratio* 38, 18, LNPF, pg. 351.
51. *Oratio* 34, 12, LNPF, pg. 337.
52. *Oratio* 31, the 5th Theological Oration on the Holy Spirit LNPF, pg. 327.

FOOTNOTES TO CHAPTER EIGHT

1. Some suggested modern works on St. Gregory of Nyssa are: Danielou, J., S. J., *Platonisme et Théologie Mystique. Doctrine Spirituelle de Saint Grégoire de Nysse*, Paris, 1944; Cherniss, H., *The Platonism of Gregory of Nyssa*, Berkeley, 1930; Koch, Hugo, *Das mystische Schauen biem hl. Gregor von Nyssa in Theologische Quartalschrift*, 1898, pg. 357 ss; Leys, Roger, S.J., *L'image de Dieu chez Saint Grégoire de Nysse*, Paris, 1951; Lieske, L., *Theologie der Christus-mystik Gregor von Nyssa in Scholastik*, 1939, pg. 484 ss; Volker, W., *Die mystik Gregors von Nyssa in ihren geschichtlichen Zusammenhangen in Theologische Zietschrift*, 1953, pg. 338 ss.; Muckle, J. S.J., *The Doctrine of S. Gregory of Nyssa on man as the image of God in Mediaeval Studies*, Toronto, 1945, VII, pgs. 55-84.
2. Danielou, J., *Grégoire de Nysse; Contemplation sur la vie de Moise in Sources Chrétiennes*, Vol. 6, Paris, 1941, pgs. 110-111.
3. Danielou, J., *Platonisme et Théologie Mystique. Doctrine Spirituelle de Saint Grégoire de Nysse*, Paris, 1944, pgs. 54-63.
4. Leys, Roger, S.J., *L'image de Dieu chez Saint Grégoire de Nysse*, Paris, 1951, pg. 99.
5. Cited by R. Leys, *op. cit.*, pg. 99.
6. *De Opificio Hominis*, Ch. 16, 1-2, cited from LNPF, Vol. 5, pg. 404.
7. *Ibid.*, pg. 405; 10-12.
8. Danielou, *Platonisme . . . op. cit.*, pg. 57.
9. *Ibid.*
10. Cf: Krampf, A., *Der Urzustand des Menschen nach die Lehre des Hl. Gregor von Nyssa*, Wurzburg, 1889, pgs. 65-66; also, R. Leys, *op. cit.*, pg. 105.
11. *De Opif. Hom.*, Ch. 16, LNPF, pg. 405.
12. Lot-Borodine, M., *La Doctrine de la deification chez les Péres grecs in Revue de l'Histoire des Religions*, T. 63, 1932, pg. 26.
13. Leys, *op. cit.*, pgs. 65-66.
14. *De Opif. Hom.*, Ch. 5, pg. 391.

15. *Op. cit.,* pg. 68.
16. *De Oratione Catech. Magna,* Ch. 5, LNPF, pgs. 479-480.
17. *De Anima et Resurrectione,* LNPF, pgs. 450-451.
18. Danielou, *Platonisme . . . op. cit.,* pgs. 55-56.
19. *De Oratione Catech. Magna,* Ch. 5, LNPF, pg. 479.
20. Messenger, E., *Evolution and Theology,* London, 1931, pgs. 23-26; 131-144.
21. *De Opif. Hom.,* Ch. 16, LNPF, pg. 406.
22. *Ibid.,* Ch. 22, 3, pg. 411.
23. *In Hexameron,* PG 44, 72-73.
24. *De Opif. Hom.,* Ch. 16, LNPF, pg. 405.
25. *Ibid.,* Ch. 17, 2, pg. 407.
26. Von Balthasar, H., *Présence et Pénsée. Essai sur la philosophie religieuse de Grégoire de Nysse,* Paris, 1942, pgs. 50-51.
27. *De Oratione Catech. Magna,* Ch. 7, LNPF, pg. 482.
28. *Ibid.,* pg. 483.
29. *De Opif. Hom.,* Ch. 22, LNPF, pgs. 411-412.
30. *De Virginitate,* PG 46,370 B.
31. *De Oratione Catech. Magna,* Ch. 9, LNPF, pgs. 484-485. Cf: also, *Contra Eunomium XII,* PG 45, 889 B; *Adversus Apollonarium,* 51, PG 45,1245 B.
32. *De Oratione Catech. Magna,* Ch. 25, LNPF, pg. 495.
33. *Homilia in Canticum XV,* PG 44,1085 B-C.
34. *Adversus Apollonarium,* PG 45, 1153 C.
35. *De Oratione Catech. Magna,* Ch. 35, LNPF, pg. 502.
36. *Ibid.,* pgs. 502-503.
37. *Ibid.,* pg. 503.
38. *Ibid.*
39. *Ibid.,* pg. 504.
40. *Contra Eunomium III,* 6, LNPF, pg. 149.
41. *De Oratione Catech. Magna,* Ch. 37, LNPF, pgs. 504-505.
42. *Ibid.,* pg. 506.
43. *De Oratione Dominica,* ACW, Vol. 18, pg. 59.
44. *De Oratione Catech. Magna,* Ch. 34, pg. 502.
45. *Ibid.,* Ch. 11, pg. 486.
46. Danielou, *Platonisme . . . . op. cit.,* pgs. 194-195.
47. PG 44,377 A-B.
48. PG 44,1001 B-C
49. *Op. cit.,* pgs. 303-307.
50. Phil. 3:13.
51. *Comm. in Canticum, Sermo 15* in *From Glory to Glory* (Texts from Gregory of Nyssa) ed. by J. Danielou and H. Musurillo, N.Y., 1961. pgs. 284-285.
52. *Ibid., Sermo 8,* pgs. 212-213.
53. *De Anima et Resurrectione,* LNPF, pg. 450.
54. *Ibid.,* pg. 468.

FOOTNOTES TO CHAPTER NINE

1. A suggested bibliography of works on St. Cyril: Burghardt, W. J., S.J., *The Image of God in Man according to Cyril*

of *Alexandria,* Wash. D.C., 1957; Du Manior, H., "Cyrille d'Alexandrie, Saint," in *Dict. de Spiritualité,* Vol. 2, 1953, 2672-83; *ibid., Dogme et spiritualité chez saint Cyrille d'Alexandrie,* Paris, 1944; Janssens, L., "Notre filiation divine d'aprés saint Cyrille d'Alexandrie" in *Ephemerides theologicae Lovanienses,* 15, 1938, pgs. 233-78; Kerrigan, A., *St. Cyril of Alexandria, Interpreter of the Old Testament,* Rome, 1952; Mahé, J., "La Sanctification d'aprés saint Cyrille d'Alexandrie" in *Revue d'histoire ecclesiastique* 10, 1909, pgs. 30-40; 469-492; *ibid.,* "Cyrille (saint), patriarche d'Alexandrie" in DTC, Vol. 3, 1908, 2476-2527; Weigl, E., *Die Heilslehre des hl. Cyrill Von Alexandrien,* Mainz, 1905.

2. Cf: Janssens, L., *art. cit.,* pg. 233; Gross, J., *op. cit.,* quotes Anastasius the Sinaite, PG 89,113 that Cyril is the "Seal of the Fathers." Cf: Quasten, *op. cit.,* Vol. 3, pg. 135; von Campenhausen, *op. cit.,* pgs. 154-155.

3. Cited by von Campenhausen, *op. cit.,* pg. 155.

4. *Ibid.*

5. Mahé, *art. cit.,* pgs. 30-40; 469-492.

6. Janssens, *art. cit.*

7. *In Ioannem* II, 8, ed. by P. E. Pusey, *Sancti patris nostri Cyrilli archiepiscopi Alexandrini in Joannis evangelium. Accedunt fragmenta varia necnon tractatus ad Tiberium diaconum duo,* 3 vols., Oxford, 1872, Vol. I, 339-40.

8. *Thesaurus* 32, PG 75,304 d; also 553; 572.

9. *Ibid.,* 13,225; *In Joan.* 6 (Pusey II,129).

10. *De sancta et consubstantiali trinitate dialogus* 5, PG 75,956.

11. *In Lucam homilia* 96, ed. by R. Payne Smith, *A commentary upon the Gospel according to St. Luke by St. Cyril,* 2, Oxford, 1859, 446, cited by Burghardt, *op. cit.,* pg. 21, ftnote 62.

12. *In Matt.,* PG 72,384.

13. *Epistola ad Calosyrium,* PG 76,1066-77.

14. Cf: what has been said above in presenting the doctrine of Athanasius and Gregory of Nyssa. Also: Bernard, R., *op. cit.,* pg. 27 and Leys, R., *op. cit.,* pgs. 116-119.

15. Cf: Weigl, E., *op. cit.,* pg. 35; Gross, J., *op. cit.,* pg. 280 and du Manoir, H., *Dogme . . . op. cit.,* pgs. 94-95.

16. De Vaux, R., "La Genese" in *La sainte Bible de Jerusalem,* Paris, 1951, pg. 42.

17. *In Psalmos,* Ps. 33, 9, PG 69,876.

18. *Responsiones ad Tiberium X* (Pusey, III,594).

19. *In Joan.* I, 9, PG 74, 145 A.

20. *Ibid., XIV,* 20,277 A-D.

21. *Glaphyra in Genesim* I, PG 69,20 B-C.

22. *Ad Calosyrium,* PG 76,1069-1072.

23. *In Joan,* XIV, 20, PG 74, 277 A-D. *In Matt.* XXIV, 51, PG 72,445 C.

24. *De trinitate dial.* IV, PG 75,908 D.

25. *Adversus Anthropomorph.* VIII, PG 76,1092 A-B.

26. *Ibid.,* X,1096.

27. *De trinitate dial.* I, PG 75,676 A.

28. Comm. In Lucam, PG 72,485 D. Cf: De recta fide ad Theodosium, PG 76, 1177 A, where Cyril says the following:
Therefore He is both the Only-begotten and the Firstborn: Only-begotten as God, but indeed Firstborn among us and among many brothers because He has become man by a mysterious union. . . . Just as it has come to pass that the humanity of Christ, because it has been united to the Word through the exchange of the Incarnation, is and is rightly called "Only-begotten", so it has become proper to the Word, which was united to flesh, to be and to be called "Firstborn" as among many brothers.

29. In Lucam, PG 72, 488 B.

30. De recta fide ad Theod., PG 76,1177 A. Similarly in the text: "Therefore is He man, made like unto us, that we might also be like unto Him. . . that we might be gods and sons," in In Joan. XX, 17, PG 74,700 B. Cf: PG 72,688 A; ibid., 688 B; PG 75,1268 C; PG 72,442 C-446 A.

31. Janssens, art. cit., pgs. 238-239.

32. De recta fide ad reginas, PG 76,1303 D-1305 A.

33. In Joan. XIV, 2, PG 74,184 B-D.

34. Cf: Janssens, art. cit., pg. 243.

35. Cf: Burghardt, op. cit., pg. 120, 112-113. He here depends on Janssens, art. cit., pgs. 275-277.

36. De recta fide ad Theod., PG 76,1177 A. Cf: for an identical passage, PG 75,1229 B.

37. Janssens, art. cit., pg. 274.

38. In Joan. XVII, 23, PG 74,564 C.

39. In Matt. XXVI, 27, PF 72,452 C.

40. In Joan. XI, 11, PG 74,560.

41. In Joan, IV, 2, PG 73, 577.

42. Von Campenhausen, op. cit., pg. 147, claims, "One third of Cyril's first work on dogmatics, the tremendous 'Thesaurus' or treasury of a true knowledge of the Holy Trinity, consists of excerpts from Athanasius' Orations."

43. Cf: Gardiel, A., "Dons du Saint Espirit" in DTC, Vol. IV, 2, 1754-1761.

44. Mahé, art. cit., pgs. 480; 475-479.

45. Ibid., pg. 480.

46. Thesaurus 34, PG 75,597 A-C.

47. Ad Serapionem I, 20 PG 26,577 B; 588 B; 592 B; IV, 3, 640 D-641 A.

48. Rom. 8:29.

49. In Joan. XVII, 18, 19, PG 74,541 C-D.

50. De Trinitate, PG 75,1088 B ss.

51. Ibid., PG 75,609-612. Cf: De recta fide ad reginas II, PG 76,1384 D.

52. In Joan. XVI, 6-7, PG 74,433 C-D. De Trinitate dial. I, PG 75,676 B.

53. In Joan. XVI, 16-17, PG 74,536 A-C.

54. In Rom. III, 21, PG 74,780 A.

55. Glaphyra in Genesim I, PG 69,20.

56. De adoratione, 2, PG 68,244.

57. Burghardt, *op. cit.*, pgs. 56-57 quotes from *In Hebraeos,*
Heb. 2:7-9 (Pusey, *In Joan.* III, pgs. 383-384).
58. *In Joan.* III, 316. Cf: *In Lucam* V, 27, PG 72,892 C.
59. *Glaphyra in Genesim,* PG 69,28.
60. *In Joan.* I, 9 (Pusey I, pg. 111).
61. *In I Cor.* VI, 15, PG 74-872 A. Cf: *Homil. Pasch.* X, PG
77,625 C-D.

FOOTNOTES TO CHAPTER TEN

1. Von Campenhausen, *op. cit.*, pg. 155.
2. *Haereses* III, 1, PG 42,341-345.
3. *Adv. Haer.*, PG 7,975.
4. Irenaeus, *Adv. Haer.* V, 6, PG 7,1138; Athanasius,
Contra Arianos III 10, PG 26,334 A.
5. Clement of Alexandria, *Strom.* VI, PG 9,317 B; *Strom.* II,
PG 8,1040 B; Origen, *De Princ.* VI, PG 11,33 C; Greg.
Nyssa, *Or. Catech.*, PG 45,21 D; Chrysostom, *In Ps.* 134,
PG 55,398. Cf: De Manoir, "Le Probleme de Dieu chez
Cyrille d'Alexandrie" in *Rech. de Sc. Relig.* XXVII, Oct.,
1937, pgs. 404-7.
6. Cf: Merki, H., *Homoiosis Theo; Von der platonischen
Angleichung an Gott zur Gottahnlichkeit bei Gregor von
Nyssa,* Freiburg, 1952, pg. 155.
7. *Surnaturel.* . . . . *op. cit;* cf: Malevez, L., "L'ésprit et le
desir de Dieu" in *Nouvelle Revue Théologique,* LXIX,
1947, pgs. 3-31. Meany, James, J., S.J., *The Image of God
in Man according to the Doctrine of St. John Damascene,*
Manila, 1954, pgs. 83-91.
8. Denielou, *Platonisme.* . . . *op. cit.*, pg. 50.
9. Crouzel, *Théologie.* . . . *op. cit.*, He notes on pgs. 161 and
163, note 104, two isolated texts where Origen implies a
distinction between nature and grace: *De Princ.* I, 3,6 and
Contra Celsum, V, 23, but such texts are indeed rare.
10. *Diadoque de Photice, Oeuvres Spirituelles* in *Sources Chrétiennes,* Vol. 5, Paris, 1955, Ch. 5, pg. 86.
11. On free will among the Greek Fathers, cf: Amand, David,
O.S.B., *Fatalisme et Liberté dans l'Antiquité Grecque,*
Louvain, 1945.
12. Evagrius, *Cap. Prac. ad Anatolium,* PG 40,1240 A. He
goes on to say that these seeds of virtue implanted in
nature can never be destroyed. The proof is Dives, even
in Hell, has pity on his brothers.
13. *Diadochus of Photice, op. cit.*, Ch. 4, pg. 86; Ch. 78, pg.
135-6; Ch. 89, pgs. 149-50.
14. Nilus, *Sermo Asceticus,* PG 79,1281 D.
15. *Epistola II,* PG 34,413 C, 412 C.
16. Cf: Hauserr, I., S.J., "L'Origine de la Theorie Orientale
des Huit Péchés Capitaux" in *Orientalia Christiana,* XXX,
Rome, 1933, pgs. 164-175. Also: Evagrius, *De Octo Vitiosis
Cogit.*, PG 40,1272-1277.
17. *Adv. Haer.* III, 19, PG 7,939 B.

18. *Ibid.,* V, 16, PG 7,1167 C.
19. *Ibid.,* IV, 38, 1108.
20. *De Orat.,* 22, PG 11,485 B-C.
21. *De Incarn. Verbi,* PG 25,192 B.
22. *In Joan.* VI, 54, PG 73,577-580; *In Joan.* XIV, 33, PG 74,473 C-D; *De Trinit.* 7, PG 75,1089 C-D.
23. *Ambig. Lib.,* PG 91,1113 B-1116 D.
24. *Op. cit.,* pg. 43.
25. Camelot, P., O.P., "La Théologie de l'Image de Dieu" in *Revue des Sciences Phil. et Théol.,* 1956, pgs. 470-471.
26. Gregory Nyssa, *De Beatitudine, Or.* VII, PG 44,1280 B-C.

MORE FINE READING AND LISTENING FROM DOVE PUBLICATIONS PECOS, NEW MEXICO 87552

DOVE PAMPHLETS

Prayer Meetings

Jim Cavnar here offers much practical advice on various types of prayer meetings. He examines, for instance, the role of leaders, the problems connected with introducing new people, the qualities a prayer meeting has when it is open to the Spirit, and dangers to avoid. Valuable reading for all members of Pentecostal prayer groups. (.35 each, $21 per 100)

Spiritual Gifts

Stephen Clark presents a straightforward and clear explanation of the nature and purpose of the nine spiritual gifts mentioned by St. Paul in I Corinthians 12: the utterance of wisdom and knowledge, faith, healing and miracles, prophecy, discernment of spirits, tongues and interpretation. Excellent instruction for newcomers to the Pentecostal experience. (.35 each, $21 per 100)

Confirmation and the "Baptism of the Holy Spirit"

Stephen Clark's thesis is that the Baptism of the Holy Spirit is an experience of the effects of Confirmation. He explains this by showing the role of faith in the reception of the sacraments. He also clarifies the reason why non-Catholics receive the "Baptism of the Holy Spirit" without receiving Confirmation. A helpful study for Catholics who are trying to place the Pentecostal experience within familiar concepts. (.25 each, $15 per 100)

The Laying on of Hands

The Pentecostal practice of laying on of hands gives rise to some questions. Father O'Connor of the University of

Notre Dame shows in this booklet that the practice does not involve superstition, nor is it a kind of pseudo-sacrament. By examining the Biblical background of this gesture, he brings out its deep spiritual meaning and the fittingness of its use by laymen and describes it as prayer in action. (.25 each, $15 per 100)

Catholic Pentecostalism: Problems in Evaluation

This is an objective, scholarly approach to Pentecostalism in general and to its impact on the Catholic mind and spirituality in particular. Its author, Father Kilian McDonnell, OSB, is the executive director of the Institute for Ecumenical and Cultural Research in Collegeville, Minnesota. He is the leading American Catholic scholar on things Pentecostal. In this booklet he offers many insights into the essence and history of Pentecostalism, its contribution to Christianity, the reasons why it is especially hard to make an unbiased judgment of it, and the problem areas that call for discerning leadership. The footnotes offer a copious bibliography. (.50 each, $30 per 100)

Pentecost in the Catholic Church

This is a trilogy of well-known articles by Father Edward O'Connor, associate professor of theology at the University of Notre Dame. "A Catholic Pentecostal Movement" has perennial interest as the first description to appear in a major magazine of the early days of Pentecostalism on the Notre Dame campus. "Pentecost and Catholicism" analyzes the essence of the Pentecostal Movement and answers some of the questions Catholics ask about its relation to their Church and the Holy Spirit. "Baptism in the Spirit: Emotional Therapy?" refutes the objection that the Pentecostal experience is merely emotional. Ideal introduction to the Catholic Pentecostal Movement. (.50 each, $30 per 100)

Baptized in the Spirit

In this 80-page booklet, Stephen Clark explains what it meant to the early Christians to be baptized in the Holy Spirit and what it means to us today. He clarifies the

218

relationship between the gift of tongues and being baptized in the Spirit. A little less than half of the booklet he devotes to understanding the experience of the Spirit as it relates to the present situation of Christians, especially those who have been leading a spiritual life without having been baptized in the Spirit in the same way as the ancient Christians. This is a long-awaited and worthy addition, to Pentecostal literature. (.60 each, $36 per 100)

Retreats and the Catholic Charismatic Renewal

From Monsignor David Rosage we have a 28-page booklet which explains the charismatic renewal and relates it to retreats. He demonstrates throughout the book that retreats and charismatic renewal share the common goal of leading a person to conversion, commitment, and contemplation. His compassion for and understanding of persons who dislike or fear any changes in liturgy, apostolates and spirituality make this an ideal introduction to the Pentecostal Movement. As a bonus, the booklet also offers the full text of the bishops' statement of 1969 and a listing of books, articles and tapes on the charismatic renewal. (.35 each, $21 per 100)

Jesus Beads

Consisting of 100 beads plus a wooden cross, Jesus Beads are a kind of rosary. They facilitate the praying of the brief "Jesus Prayer," of which there exist several versions. In this booklet, Fr. David Geraets, Doctor of Missiology and abbot of the Pecos Benedictine Abbey, expounds on a method of prayer which enriches our spirit, soul and body. There is much light here on the prayer of empathy, spontaneous and transcendental prayer, and on the relationship between prayer and the charisms of revelation, prophecy, wisdom, knowledge and healing. (.60 each, $36 per 100)

Growing in the Spirit

George Martin's writings have been guiding Christians for years. This booklet brings together 25 meditations which originally appeared in the Lansing, Michigan, Day of Renewal Notes. Containing ever timely advice and insight, they focus on key aspects of our response to the free gift of God's love and loving Spirit. (.50 each, $30 per 100)

The Age of the Spirit

In this 70-page booklet, Verla Mooth presents a wealth of scripture teaching. She begins by examining the import of the Old Testament references to the Spirit of God, then moves into the New Testament, giving special attention to the meaning of Pentecost. The second half of the work explains what all this implies for the Church and each Christian: the Baptism in the Spirit, the fullness of the Spirit, and the gifts and fruits of the Spirit. Here is a treasure trove of information about the Age of the Spirit in which we now live. (.60 each, $36 per 100)

Mary Is Pentecostal

For those who think that there is no room for Mary, the mother of Jesus, in the charismatic movement, this pamphlet may prove an eye-opener. For those who are searching for a balanced charismatic view of Mary, here is a good place to begin. The co-authors approach the topic frankly and interestingly, Larry Alberts (pastoral coordinator of the Body of Christ Covenant Community in Grand Forks, ND) sharing his personal experiences and Fr. Louis Pfaller (Assumption Abbey, Richardton, ND) sketching a biblical theology of Mary's role in the kingdom. (.60 each, $36 per 100)

Relating to the Spiritual World

As more and more people become aware of the reality and power of the spiritual realm, the need for practical guidance in relating to this realm increases. Morton Kelsey, scholarly author of several important books on the divine encounter, healing, dreams and tongue-speaking, provides twelve guidelines which every serious seeker can make use of. These are suggestions for action that spell out exactly what we can and must do. Every Christian will want to have this pamphlet for study and reference. (.60 each, $36 per 100)

DOVE CASSETTES

Pentecostal Witness
>   by Fr. George Maloney, S.J. (1 tape) $6.95

The Jesus Prayer
>   by Fr. George Maloney, S.J. (1 tape) $6.95

Prayer As Listening
>   by Fr. George Maloney, S.J. (1 tape) $6.95

Man: The Icon of God
>   by Fr. George Maloney, S.J. (1 tape) $6.95

The Logos and the Secular City
>   by Fr. George Maloney, S.J. (1 tape) $6.95

A Portrait of Jesus Christ in Music
>   by the Trees Group (1 tape) $4.00

A Pentecostal Retreat
>   by Abbot David Geraets, OSB (8 tapes) $20.00

A Pentecostal Biblical Weekend on St. John
>   by Fr. Jim Wolff (7 tapes) $17.50

A Pentecostal Biblical Weekend on the Eucharist
>   by Fr. Jim Wolff (4 tapes; 7 talks) $10.00

DOVE LEAFLETS

Sold in bulk only:

> 50-99 of one title: 10¢ each.
> 100-499 of one title: 9¢ each.
> 500-999 of one title: 8¢ each.
> 1000 of one title. 7¢ each.

Baptism in the Holy Spirit
    by Jim Scully

Go . . . Speak in Tongues
    (a meditation) by Catherine Doherty

So You've been Baptized in the Holy Spirit!
What Next?
    by Abbot David Geraets

Charismatic Renewal
    by Jim Scully

The Catholic Pentecostal Movement
    by Jim Scully

Holy Spirit: Purity and Power
    by Verla Mooth

The Coming of the Comforter
    by Verla Mooth

The Gift of Tongues
    by Jim Scully

(Prices subject to change)

For postage and handling kindly include 30 cents on orders up to $5.00. For orders over $5.00 include 10% of the total. All orders must be prepaid. Thank You.